How to Excel at
Distributor Sales

- David Kahle -

To Jim
a great distributor rep!

Dave Kahle

How to Excel at
Distributor Sales

Winning strategies for distributor and dealer salespeople facing a competitive environment.

- David Kahle -

The DaCo Corporation
PO Box 230017 • Grand Rapids, MI 49523

How to Excel at Distributor Sales
Copyright © 1995 David Kahle

ISBN: 0-9647042-0-X

Library of Congress Catalog Card Number: 95-69823

Cover Design:
John Fetter Advertising / Design

Illustrations:
Michael A. VanderWall, Graphic Design
Cristal Shaw, In-House Graphics

Type design and electronic publishing:
Chris Willis, Media 1

First Edition, First Printing August, 1995
Printed in the United States of America

The DaCo Corporation
PO Box 230017 • Grand Rapids, MI 49523
1.800.331.1287 • Fax: 616.451.9412

Acknowledgments

The concepts, strategies and techniques in this book evolved from a number of different sources. I am grateful to each for their contributions.

This book is a direct result of the experiences I've had with hundreds of customers and manufacturers during my tenure as a distributor salesperson. It was my experience with them that provided the raw material for this book.

The input I've received from years of work with my clients has helped me prioritize and refine that material. Their honest interaction has been incredibly valuable.

The dialogue I've had with thousands of salespeople who have participated in my seminars has helped me refine and focus those ideas.

Supporting me in all of this has been the understanding and encouragement of my wife, Coleen, all the kids, and an exceptionally capable and loyal assistant, Jessica Swenson.

Undergirding all of my experiences has been the impact of Jesus Christ on my life. It has been my encounter with Him that has brought direction and purpose in my life.

Finally, I must make special, post-humus acknowledgment of the contribution made by Ned Shaheen, the best manager I ever worked for. It was Ned who, years ago, urged me to "write the book on distributor sales."

Table of Contents

Introduction

The distribution industry has more challenge, opportunity and reward for the professional salesperson than any other.

That's the conclusion I came to while I was working as a sales recruiter for a large agency in the suburbs of Detroit. I disliked all the hours in the office that came with the sales recruiting business. So, I was determined to get back to an outside sales position where I was most comfortable.

But, before I started to circulate my resume, I decided to make use of my privileged position to analyze different sales situations and find the one that offered the right ingredients. At that point in my life, this meant the opportunity to make a lot of money with unlimited potential, very little travel, and the opportunity to settle down and grow with one company.

As a sales recruiter, I enjoyed an insider's perspective on the career paths open to a professional salesperson. I learned, for example, that there was *always* a lot of money to be made with a new manufacturer with some hot new technology. However, the opportunities didn't last long, and as soon as the market was established, the highly-compensated salespeople gave way to lower-paid salespeople. Larger, well-established companies offered stability, but generally limited the amount of money you could make. And, if you weren't interested in travel, then climbing the career ladder as sales manager, district manager, and so on, was not an option.

That's when I discovered distribution. I saw it as an opportunity to make a lot of money, to be relatively independent, to minimize my travel, and to settle in with a company for the duration.

I eventually wound up as a salesperson with a growing distributor. It's then that my appreciation for distribution began. I spent the next five years traveling the northern suburbs of Detroit selling hospital supplies. As I look back on my career, it was a time in my life when I probably learned more than in any other comparable period of time. I experienced some of my most horrendous failures – those lessons that you learn once and never want to learn again. But, I also had some of my greatest successes, made more money, created more friends, and had more contacts than at any other time in my career.

I became the number one salesperson for that company, producing a million dollar a year increase for each of five years in an industry where a million dollar territory separated the men from the boys.

From there, I accepted a promotion to become the general manager of a start-up division of a distributor. That business grew from nothing to over $200,000 in monthly sales in just 38 months, selling exclusively through distributors. In that experience, I saw the situation from the perspective of a "manufacturer," someone who depends on distributors to market and distribute the product.

Since 1988, I have been in private practice as a consultant, speaker and a sales trainer, working primarily with distributors and manufacturers who sell through distributors.

Over the years, I've come to thoroughly enjoy distribution. I love the action, the thousand balls you can keep in the air, and the dynamics on both sides of the equation – customers and manufacturers.

In this book, I will share with you some of the things that I have learned along the way.

First, you will acquire some powerful concepts regarding successful distributor sales strategies. Even if all you do is skim through the highlights of this book, you'll gain some concepts for effective distributor sales that will make a real difference in your performance.

Second, you will understand how to maintain a positive attitude. I understand that sales is a difficult and lonely business. You may occasionally feel frustrated and depressed. I hope that as a result of reading this book you may begin to feel that you really do have the ability to positively impact what you do. You *can* make a positive difference, and you can feel a little bit more positive about yourself and your job.

Third, you will find several key, practical ideas that you can put to use right away. Regardless of whether you choose to implement the entire system this book discusses or not, you can still garner specific ideas and tactics that *will* make you more effective.

Finally, you will discover a system for personally improving your behavior so that you can become a star salesperson. For those of you motivated and driven to success, I offer you a comprehensive system of personal improvement in all the important areas of your job. If you implement the total system, I have no doubt that you'll excel at distributor sales.

In addition to this book, I have developed a number of

resources to help those of you who are serious about growing as salespeople. They include the audio cassette tape training course, "How To Become a Master of Distribution Sales," which is described on page 269. In addition, there are three self-contained, programmed manuals which are designed to help you gain mastery of a specific area. The three include: "How To Master Time and Territory Management," "How To Overcome Objections," and "Systematically Improving Your Performance." You'll find these described on page 270.

For sales managers, vice-presidents of sales, and owners, we offer an additional set of resources. These include a leaders' guide for "How To Become a Master of Distribution Sales." This manual allows you to turn the program into a four -to-ten session small group training program. "How To Use Telemarketing to Increase Profits in Your Distribution Business" is a cassette tape program that describes all the details necessary to successfully manage this often underestimated task. "How To Find, Interview, Select and Hire a Good Salesperson," is the most comprehensive, powerful program of its kind, designed to help you make one of your most difficult decisions. These programs are described on page 269.

Finally, we provide in-house seminars and training programs ranging from short keynote presentations to customized videotape training sessions. To inquire about those, or to ask any questions about the material in this text, call me at 800-331-1287, or fax to 616-451-9412.

Dave Kahle
The DaCo Corporation
PO Box 230017 • Grand Rapids, MI 49523
1.800.331.1287 • Fax: 616.451.9412

Chapter 1
Turbulent Times

Last week one of my friends shocked me by announcing that he had to get out of the business he owned and find another one.

I was stunned. My first thought was, "Why on earth would he need to find a different business?" Chuck was living the American dream. Ten years ago he was a computer repairman who risked everything by leaving his job to develop his own computer repair business. Over the past seven years, Chuck had built an efficient, productive business employing 15 people in two locations.

His business was stable and profitable, he was well regarded by his clients, he had a good, loyal group of employees, and he was enjoying an income probably greater than he had ever imagined.

He was relishing the kind of situation most people only dream about. So why did he need to find a new business?

Here's what he told me. "In five years I'll be out of business. Manufacturers are continually building computers that are smaller, cheaper and more reliable. It won't be long before you won't repair them — you'll throw them away like you do a toaster."

Chuck's business was a winner in an industry — micro computer repair — that will have come and gone in a period of about fifteen years. No matter how effective and productive Chuck was as a businessman, the rapid changes in our economy mean that the long-term prospect for his business was dim. And Chuck was astute enough to recognize that before it was too late.

Unfortunately, rapid change is the rule today, not the exception. And it's just one element of several that combine to make the 1990s one of the most difficult times our nation's businesses have ever seen.

Howard Stein said, "All I know is, things don't work like they used to work. So don't plan on doing anything based on the past." [1]

The sentiments he expressed could have been voiced by almost every businessperson I know. It's as if some sinister spirit were prowling through our economy, rendering all the wisdom of the past useless, and casting a spell of confusion and uncertainty over the land.

Business is not like it used to be — even just a few years ago. It's important for us to know why this is the case, so we can confront and conquer that demon.

I've noted five major trends surging with irresistible power through our society . These trends are powerful forces which combine to threaten the existence of every distributor.

Like a river with strong currents that twist and surge to form powerful whirlpools that pull everyone they touch to their doom, so these trends are like five currents which converge to propel distributors into a whirlpool of confusion and uncertainty.

Let's take a look at each of the five currents.

---

1. *As quoted in The Intuitive Manager. Roy Rowan. Little, Brown and Co., 1986*

The First Current:
Rapid, Discontinuous Change

Our society and our business environment are changing more rapidly than at any time in our history. Not only that, but the pace of change is itself increasing.

We've always had change. In fact, change may be a definition for life itself. If you're not changing, you're probably dead! I recall, in my days as a distributor salesperson, being very frustrated with one account. The account had a prime vendor relationship with my arch competitor and, no matter what I did, I couldn't increase my meager business there. I ended up venting my frustrations to my manager who counseled me to "hang in there."

"The only thing you can be sure of," he said, "is that things will change. You need to position yourself to take advantage of those changes when they happen." Events proved him right. My competitor changed salespeople, experienced some service problems, and I had the opening I was waiting for.

So, we've always had change. What's different now is the rate of change. Things are changing more rapidly than ever before.

Consider this. In 1900, the total amount of knowledge available to mankind doubled about every 500 years. Today, it doubles about every two years. That incredibly rapid pace of new knowledge production infuses energy into the forces of change at an unprecedented rate.

It's not knowledge that causes change, it's the application of knowledge. We see the application of knowledge in new products, new technologies, new customers, new needs — all coming at an increasingly rapid rate.

Like it or not, the conclusions, paradigms and core beliefs

upon which we based our decisions two years ago are likely to be obsolete today.

Chuck's story is a good example. Two years ago the future looked great for his business. Today, it looks dim. Things have changed. And these changes came about as a result of increased knowledge on the part of the computer manufacturers. Think about it. An IBM PC was worth about $4,500 when it was introduced a few years ago. Today, it probably doesn't even have scrap value. Things changed. The application of increased knowledge resulted in new products which made that product obsolete.

If that was true for the IBM PC, think about what may happen to today's hot product. Regardless of how well researched, engineered and manufactured it may be, it could become obsolete and worthless in two years!

One futurist has predicted that, by the year 2020, knowledge will increase at an astounding rate — doubling every 35 days! What that means for distributors is that the rapid change affecting almost every aspect of your business — products, markets, customers, etc. — will only continue to increase in speed.

In almost every seminar I've presented over the last few years I've asked the question, "Are things changing more rapidly in your business today than they did three years ago?" In a show of hands, almost 100 percent of the participants say "Yes."

I'll ask you to consider the same question. Are things changing more rapidly in your business today than they did three years ago?

Now consider one more question. Do you expect the rate of change to continue to increase, or to slow down in the near future? The answer's obvious. We are living in a world that is changing more rapidly than anything mankind has experienced ever before.

But there's another element to this current of rapid change. Not only is change in the 1990s rapid, but it's unlike anything we've seen before.

Charles Handy, in his book, *The Age of Unreason*, makes a convincing argument that change today is "discontinuous." In other words, it doesn't necessarily evolve out of patterns or trends that we can predict.

For example, the three television networks co-existed quite comfortably for years. They competed with one another and gradually changed as the technology and tastes of their audience evolved.

But then, in a matter of a year or two, cable television burst onto the field, and the networks suddenly had hundreds of small stations and networks to do battle with.

Their world was turned upside down by a technological development which changed things in a "discontinuous" fashion.

The Second Current: Relentlessly Growing Complexity

The explosion in knowledge means that the products we buy and sell are becoming increasingly complex.

Automobiles are a good example. Last spring one of our family cars stopped running. It didn't gradually slow down or signal it's impending demise by running roughly — it just stopped. Suddenly and without advance warning. It was as if it just announced one day, "I will run no more," and then shut itself down.

No matter what I did, I couldn't get it to start. A look under the hood revealed a complex array of wires and tiny black boxes that were totally new to me. Automobiles had become so complex that I had no idea what those little electronic boxes did. Nor how to fix them.

Just a few years ago that maze of wires and electronics would not have been there, and the car wouldn't have been nearly so intimidating. I could have wiggled a wire, adjusted a carburetor, or done *something* to revive it.

But the explosion of knowledge and the resulting complexity in my car left me intimidated and totally confused by what I saw under the hood.

So, in frustration, I gave up and had the car towed to the dealer. And what did the dealer do to it? The mechanic hooked it up to a computer to tell him what was wrong. The car had become so complex that even the mechanic couldn't diagnose the problem without the assistance of a computer.

Are we that many years away from the trusty mechanic at the corner service station who could diagnose the problem by listening to the purr or grumble of the engine? Yes. And no.

Yes — because those days are gone forever. The complexity we're building into today's automobiles means that mechanics, computers, and highly trained specialists are the only way we are going to be able to effectively deal with these machines in the future.

And no — it's only been a few years since the system that had served us so well since the advent of the mass produced automobile became a vestige of the past, a victim of rapid change and growing complexity.

It's another example of Chuck's computer repair business. Dealt a death blow by rapid, discontinuous change and growing complexity.

Answer this simple question. Have the products or services you sell become noticeably more complex over the last three years?

I have yet to have anyone tell me "no" in answer to that

question.

But product complexity is only one part of the relentlessly growing complexity current.

It is becoming more and more difficult to manage a business because of the complexity that comes as a result of government regulation. Despite twelve years of Republican presidents — men sworn to pursue the benefits of de-regulation — the amount of complex regulation that business and organizations have to contend with has expanded geometrically.

Think of the great tax reform act of 1990. Or, the Americans with Disabilities Act which ushered in an entirely new area of regulation. The number of regulations that business people are expected to follow only continues to grow. So much so that a survey conducted by Newstrack Executive Tape Service found that 54 percent of the CEOs and senior executives surveyed listed regulation among their top 3 challenges.

My business is about as small as they come. Two full-time employees, an occasional temporary part-time employee, and a bevy of associates who are subcontractors on an as needed basis. At the end of the last quarter, my accountant presented me with 20 pages of reports I had to sign and then mail to various regulating and taxing agencies, and six checks to write to those same agencies. And that was just the quarterly report of a tiny, essentially one-man practice!

Is it any wonder that the ranks of the professional regulation handlers — accountants, attorneys, and consultants — continue to grow?

One last source of complexity — our friends the attorneys. It seems that with every new law school graduate, the chances of getting sued for something increase. And with every lawsuit we read about or hear about, we, of necessity, become more defensive in our practices. Thus the number of "de facto" regulations we must confront grows exponentially.

George Will, writing in *Newsweek* magazine, quotes the Wall Street Journal:

> *In California, lawyers prowl outside factories after layoffs have been announced, trying to recruit stress cases. Workers only have to claim that 10 percent of their anxiety is job-related to collect benefits. One L.A. clinic even offers the worker's comp equivalent of frequent flyer miles — a free trip to Las Vegas for anybody who visited the clinic 30 times in three months.*

With the US claiming 70 percent of the world's lawyers, the prospect is great for this current to continue to swell. Add this all together, and we get a picture of the businessman weighted down by the tentacles of growing complexity all around him.

But don't take my word for it. Assess your own situation. Reflect on these two simple questions.

Is your business more complex today than it was three years ago?

Do you expect things to get simpler or more complex in the future? The answers are almost universally the same.

The Third Current: Constantly Growing Competition/Choices

As a vendor, do you have more competition today than you did three years ago? As a consumer, do you have more choices today than you did a few years ago?

Last summer my wife went to Florida for three weeks to help care for her ill father. That left me home with three of the kids. And that meant grocery shopping.

It had been a number of years since I seriously entered the grocery store in search of the family's weekly provisions. I had, of course, run in from time to time to pick up the miscellaneous one or two items that we needed for a special meal or which we had inadvertently run out of in the middle of a recipe. But I hadn't really had the responsibility for bringing back the week's groceries.

The cereal aisle was a revelation. Stacked from the floor to above my head, running the length of the entire row, were literally hundreds of choices in cereal. I was confused and overwhelmed. I didn't have time to read all the box labels, and every package was designed to pull my attention to it. I threw my hands up in frustration, and bought a box of Shredded Wheat!

My very real frustration with all the choices I had was a simple illustration of the third current surging relentlessly through our society — constantly growing competition and choices.

The overwhelming number of choices that I faced in that grocery aisle wasn't an isolated instance. In almost every area we look at, under every nook and cranny of our economy, we are faced with an explosion of choices.

It wasn't so long ago that we had a choice of a handful of TV stations. Today we can choose from at least 40.

There are two sides to this current. On the one hand, it represents increased choices and freedom for consumers. On the other, increased competition for vendors.

Competition is increasing for several reasons. First, the slowdown in the growth of the American economy after the rapid growth of the '80s has meant that most companies are no longer experiencing the growth they enjoyed in the '80s. For a time, it seemed that all you had to do was open your doors and you'd experience a 20 percent annual growth rate. So, in searching for the growth that stockholders have come to expect, your traditional competitors have ventured into new geographical areas or new vertical markets. The competitor on the other side of the state, for example, may now be sending a salesperson into your area — an area they were content to leave alone in the past. Or that industrial distributor headquartered down the street from you is taking on new product lines that compete with yours, where before he was content to stick to the product category he did the best with. That's the first source of increasing competition.

Second, there's the new competition from alternate sources. The discount warehouse, mail order cataloger, or telemarketing operation that offers new choices to your customers — other ways to acquire the same products.

The technology revolution means that more and more processes are being "computerized" and the local computer consultant may be offering alternate ways for your customer to handle the same processes.

Third, as America goes through the downsizing trend in response to increased competition, it creates even more competition. Many of the hundreds of thousands of laid-off white collar workers will not find gainful employment in the industry that they left. Their survival strategy will be to start their own businesses.

In 1987, the number of business owners surpassed the number of union members in this country. The curves now are moving farther and farther apart. This means (from a competitive perspective) that there are more new businesses being formed all of the time and, thus, more and more competition and choices for your customers.

Here's another source of increasing competition — overseas competitors. As the world becomes smaller due to improved transportation and communication technology, foreign competitors are entering our markets. I have yet to work with an industry that didn't have a relatively new foreign player involved.

Finally, our rapidly growing knowledge means innovations in technology. And that technology means new choices for consumers, and new sources of competition for vendors.

Ask yourself these simple questions. Do you have more competition today than you had a few years ago? Do you expect to see more competition in the future?

The Fourth Current: Constraints on Time

A friend called my wife and me with an invitation to spend an evening together. As we compared calendars, we discovered that it was three weeks before both of us had an evening free!

Unfortunately, that was no isolated event. Our lives have become so full, and so scheduled, that we have very little "free time." And I believe we're very typical.

Franklin Planners have become ubiquitous in business circles — a symptom of the growing number of commitments we make. When was the last time you made an appointment with someone who didn't have to wade through pages of commitments in an elaborately detailed calendar? As we've become more aware of time, and more committed to using it wisely, we also use it more fully, and leisure time is rapidly becoming a more scarce and precious commodity.

According to those who study such things, the average American works 158 more hours per year than he did 20 years ago.[2] That's almost one full month more! Unfortunately, work time is increasing at the expense of family and leisure time.

---

2. *Research Reports, February 24, 1992.*

And our guilt is rising in direct proportion — we're all trying to cram more productivity into the time we have. The extra hours and leisure minutes we used to use to consider some strategy or situation have disappeared. We're in the quick solution, fire fighting mode — all due to the increasing pressure on our time.

But, regardless of what is happening to other people, the really important question is, "Is this happening to you?"

Ask yourself this question. "Do I have more pressure on my time today than I did a few years ago?" And, if so, "Do I realistically expect to get more time, or less time, in the near future?"

If your answer to the last question is "less time," then you have a problem. You have a more difficult, more confusing economy to deal with, and you have less time in which to do it.

The Fifth Current:
Crush of Information

What ever happened to the predictions of a paperless office?

I don't know about you, but I'm using more paper than I ever have — reams and reams of it. And most of it is being produced by that malevolent little blinking machine that was supposed to eliminate it all — the desktop computer.

I suspect that my office is similar to yours. You're probably using more paper than ever. There's fax paper, computer paper, laser computer paper, copy paper, etc.

All this is symptomatic of the growing weight of information that is threatening to smother all of us.

Never before have we had so much information to contend with.

Computer programs have been developed that allow us to create information that we never thought of before. We can sort a database in so many different ways that we can find combinations of demographics we didn't even know existed. And pages and pages of information can be produced at the touch of a button that before were almost impossible to create.

For example, I get regular mailings from an organization which calls itself the Institute for Data-based Marketing. This association organizes an annual convention attended by thousands of devotees. Here is an association serving an industry totally devoted to the intricacies of using new kinds of information. Not only is the industry itself new, but the information product which gives it its definition didn't even exist a few years ago.

Another new industry is emerging — information brokering. A hybrid combination of database marketing and list brokering, this industry emerged only a couple of years ago.

As a result of this technological innovation, we have more information available to us in our offices than we have had ever before.

I was recently involved in a project to revise the sales and marketing system for the parts department of a major international manufacturer. As part of my standard procedures, I created a questionnaire for the supervisors to complete. On the day I was to receive the responses to the questionnaire, I was surprised to find a UPS delivery rather than a manila envelope in the mail. The responses to my questions consisted of about 8 inches of computer print-outs!

We are confronted with so much information that it is overwhelming. How do we sift through and make sense of all this stuff? In your job, do you have more information coming at you today than you did a few years ago? If so, you have a problem — how are you going to sort through all this in order to get usable information? You need to develop a systematic way of managing the flood of information available to you. Otherwise you'll be overwhelmed by it.

These five currents are swirling through our society creating whirlpools of confusion and uncertainty — an incredibly turbulent time. Salespeople for distributors of every size and type — like you — are being overwhelmed by these forces. The net result? You can no longer do business the way you did a few years ago.

By reading this book, and taking the time to implement it's concepts and tactics, you will gain control over the five currents, and learn to excel at distributor sales. You'll learn to successfully deal with our turbulent economy.

To implement the ideas in this chapter...

Anticipate the growing turbulence in your industry by considering these questions:

1. What changes do you anticipate happening in the next three years in:

    • The products you sell?

    • The customers you serve?

    • The technologies you sell?

    • The processes within your company?

2. What areas of your job will grow more complex over the next three years?

3. What can you do about that now to gain mastery of that complexity?

4. From what sources do you anticipate more competition over the next few years?

5. What can you do now to prepare for it?

6. How do you see the growing pressure to produce more in less time affecting you and your customers?

7. What can you do about it now?

8. How extensively do you see the crush of information affecting you in the next few years?

9. What can you do about it now?

Chapter Two
Your Strategic Advantage In The Information Age

One of my clients told me about an occasion where he introduced himself to a young lady at a cocktail party. In the course of the conversation, the lady asked, "What do you do?" He said he owned a distribution company. She remarked, "Oh, you're a middleman." He said "Yes, I'm one of those blood-sucking middlemen who cause everything to be higher priced."

That may be one way of looking at the industry and, unfortunately, it's a perspective encouraged by the popular media. I prefer to think of distribution companies and distributor sales people as bridge builders who provide a very valuable function.

Distributors bring people together with the products they need — and they do it effectively and economically. Manufacturers often can't economically get to their customers without distributors. And, customers often can't get the products they need economically without distributors. For example, imagine that you're a retailer of office supplies. You're one of thousands of office supply retailers in this country. If you had to go directly to every manufacturer of every product line you carried, you'd probably have to make 1,000 phone calls to place orders every month. Imagine what that would cost in time as well as money.

On the other hand, suppose you're a manufacturer of paper clips, and you need to sell to every retail office supply store in the country. Can you imagine what it would cost you to visit each store and convince them to stock your paper clips?

One of the best ways for a customer to economically access a wide variety of products from different manufacturers is through a distributor. And, one of the best ways for a manufacturer to economically reach all of its potential customers is through a distributor. Both sides of this powerful marketing equation revolve around an effective distributor.

This equation is now being threatened by the five currents of change presented in Chapter One. The traditional role of the distributor is changing. At the same time, the value brought to the customer is also changing.

Many manufacturers are aggressively moving to service the largest customers themselves. They often justify this on the basis of increasing their gross profit or of meeting their customer's demands for price concessions.

Advances in computer and telecommunications technology have been used by other manufacturers to bypass the traditional distributor. One manufacturer of industrial products recently consolidated its warehouses into one central, national location, and made a deal with an air freight company to ship overnight, anywhere in the country, for about 1/2 the going rate. With that kind of system, the customer can acquire the product just as quickly from a manufacturer as he can from a local stocking distributor.

Add to that the explosion of direct marketing efforts resulting from advances in database technology. It's now much easier for a manufacturer to keep track of customers around the country, and to design precise marketing and sales programs to target multiple market segments.

But it's not just manufacturers who are threatening the traditional distributor. New competitors are cropping up in almost every product category, nibbling away at the customers of the traditional distributor. Telemarketers and mail order companies are rapidly expanding. One of my clients indicated that his business of distributing medical products to nursing homes was being attacked by a cataloger selling over the phone from three states away.

In this kind of environment, what advantage do you have? In other words, what value can you bring the customer that is worth him doing business with you instead of someone else?

When I've asked that question in my distributor sales seminars, I've listened to a number of good responses.

One participant said, "Your competitive edge is less dependent on the product you sell, and more dependent on the people and the services you provide."

That's *real* insight. In a world where the customer can buy the same product from a number of other people, the product becomes less important than the people and the services that may come with that product. A distributor can bring added value to his customers through quality people and services.

Another said, "In today's market, a distributor can more effectively reduce the number of vendors a customer uses." He was looking at the situation from the customer's point of view. His point is that a distributor can reduce the number of vendors that a particular end user has to deal with. Most customers work toward that end, believing that fewer vendors equals lower costs. A distributor is positioned to do that in a way that most manufacturers aren't. Because most distributors carry multiple lines, they can provide more of a customer's needs, and thus assist them in reducing the number of vendors used.

Not only can a distributor be effective in reducing the number of suppliers a customer uses, but he can also use his broader product knowledge to more completely fill his customers' needs.

Here's another great insight from a seminar participant. "The success of a distribution organization, and the individual salesperson, is tied directly to the success of your customer."

Manufacturers generally have more superficial relationships with a larger number of customers, while distributors generally create more in-depth relationships with fewer customers. It's not unusual for a manufacturer's salesperson to have a territory in which there may be 10 to 30 distributor reps. Warehouse clubs and mail order houses don't build deep relationships with anyone, and no one customer is that important to their business. Obviously, the traditional distributors are going to have opportunities for greater, deeper relationships with customers. Their success is closely tied to the success of their customers.

Look for the threads that tie these characteristics together and your strategic advantages become easier to see. Distributors — you — can develop deeper relationships with your customers than much of your competition. You're closer to the customer and you see him more often. You know your customer more deeply, more broadly and in a more detailed way than anyone else. The ability to know your customer better can be your biggest advantage.

But that's only the first part of the equation. Since you know your customer better, you can combine your broad product knowledge and your experience in product applications with your ability to provide unique services. In other words, you can create powerful solutions and systems for your customers.

When you do this, you create a valuable relationship where your customer comes to see you as a business partner — an almost indispensable part of his business. Illustration # 1 graphically represents this equation.

Distributor's Strategic Advantage

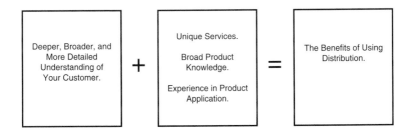

Illustration #1

That brings us to you. You now need to consider these questions personally. What unique value can you bring to your customers? Why should they buy from you instead of someone else?

First, let's analyze the unique position you occupy. Remember, you're the key to holding all of this together. You're the hub of the wheel. You're the essential center around which much of the economy's transactions revolve.

Think of yourself as being the person in the middle (Illustration # 2). On one side are the people who comprise the "front end" of your job. They are the purchasing agents, end users, department heads, engineers, supervisors, and foremen — all the various decision makers who are involved in the decision to purchase and use the products you sell. They count

The Distributor Salesperson - In the Middle

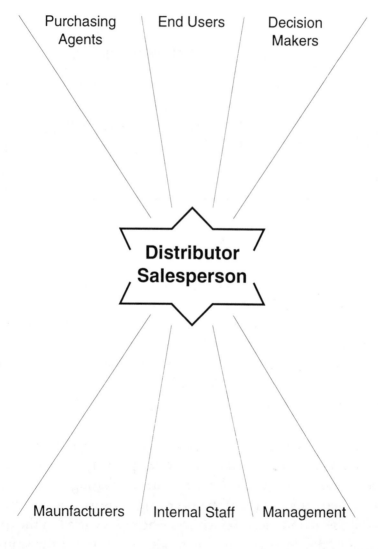

Illustration #2

on you to inform and educate them about products and services they can use. They look to you to present solutions to their problems.

On the other side are the people on the "back end" of your job. They are the manufacturers you represent and, in a similar sense, your internal staff and management. You're between all of this. Both sides depend on you to bring everyone together.

This has profound implications. With a multiple line of products, often in the thousands, selling a particular product is less important than convincing the customer to buy *something*.

The priority changes. Manufacturers focus on selling *their products*. Distributors focus on keeping the customer sold. It's not a play on words — it's a significant paradigm difference. Instead of revolving around the product, the way a manufacturer does, the distributor revolves around the customer. The product is secondary.

And therein lies your unique strategic advantage, and the value you bring the customer. Your customers can get the product, delivered on time and with accuracy from other sources. What you alone can offer are:

1. The ability to know your customer more deeply and more broadly than any other competitive source.

2. Deeper relationships.

3. Broad product knowledge which can translate itself into efficient and effective applications for the customer.

4. Finally, in today's rapidly changing world, you can make change work for you by becoming the source of applied knowledge for your customer. When dozens of new products are introduced every year, how is your customer going to learn about

them? You're perfectly positioned to sell your applied product knowledge to him.

All of this means that you, the distributor salesperson, are going to have to think about your job differently. Instead of seeing yourself as a seller of product, you need to see yourself as a provider of information, solutions and systems. You need to begin by changing your paradigms.

The Distributor Salesperson in The Information Age

The transition in our economy from the Industrial Age to the Information Age requires that you're going to have to think about your job differently. Not only must you think differently, but you must act on those new thoughts in a more disciplined fashion then ever before.

Too many distributor salespeople have the image of themselves as "good old boys." They are friendly, service-oriented people who travel a route and often check inventories, see how many pieces are left in the bin, and ask "What do you need today?" Their primary purpose is to build friendly relationships with their customers and pick up orders. They see a lot of people and sell a lot of stuff.

The Information Age, however, requires a different role for the distributor salesperson. You must see yourself as more professional, systematic and disciplined then ever before. You must still see your customers frequently, but now your calls have to be focused and disciplined. You still need to build relationships, but you understand that a major part of that relationship comes from the economic value you're able to bring to your customer. You must be a source of information focused on how your customer can derive value from the products and solutions you sell. You rarely pick up orders, understanding that is a function better performed by customer service, or EDI. Instead, you see yourself as a consultant, bringing powerful, useful information to your customers.

You build deeper relationships, based on solid economic value, with fewer customers. And avoiding non-productive activities, you become far more productive to your company, and you make more money then you ever did.

The transition can be confusing. When you look out at the world, you find an increasingly turbulent situation. When you look at your job, you see the unique nature of the industry. The natural question is, where do you fit in? What do you need to do to survive and prosper in these turbulent times?

In order to implement these four strategic advantages, you need to be good in six different areas. I call these the six essential competencies for distributor sales people.

These competencies describe the profile of the most effective distributor sales people. They also provide a model, or a standard for you to strive for as you shape your efforts at self-improvement.

The Six Essential Competencies

1. Organizing Yourself. Begin with the number of prospects and customers in your territory. Multiply that by the number of individual decision makers, influencers, gatekeepers, and end users within each account. Multiply that by the number of products your company offers. Factor in the number of manufacturer's reps you must deal with.

That begins to give you an idea of the complexity of the distributor salesperson's job. No wonder the first step is organizing yourself so that you can make sense out of all of this.

2. Building Relationships. Because distributors generally sell a large number of line items to a relatively small group of customers, they see those customers over and over again. More than any other type of selling situation, distributor salespeople need to develop deeper and broader relationships with those customers.

It's not unusual, in fact, for a significant amount of business to be awarded simply on the basis of the relationship the salesperson has developed with the customer. This is particularly true when there are a number of distributors vying for the same piece of business, and all have the same product line.

When everything else is perceived to be about the same by a customer, the order will generally go to the salesperson who has developed the strongest relationship with the buyer.

3. Transferable sales skills. There was a time when distributor salespeople didn't need any sales skills. It seemed like their job was limited to visiting customers, drinking coffee together, and picking up orders. The distributor wasn't really expected to actually *sell something.*

Those days are rapidly coming to an end in some industries, and have long since past in most. As competitive pressures have increased and margins fallen, it is no longer economically viable to pay a person just to visit customers and pick up orders.

It's essential for the distributor salesperson to master a set of templates and processes that he can transfer from product to product, manufacturer to manufacturer, situation to situation — a set of basic tools.

Distributor salespeople must understand sales presentations and sales theory better than other salespeople. Other salespeople can take the time to learn how to sell their product. Distributor salespeople have to learn how to sell anything.

4. Controlling Yourself. Half of a salesperson's job is working with people — interacting with customers and prospects. That's what we talk about the most, and that's the area we focus on. However, the other half is just as important. The other half is working with yourself.

It's been my observation that the biggest obstacles to success lie within our own heads. We develop frustration and depression. We begin to think negatively and procrastinate. We don't discipline ourselves to do the things we need to do. As a result of these internal problems, we're not as successful as we could be.

In our highly competitive world, a salesperson needs every advantage available. Most of those begin internally.

5. Working smart by planning and preparing. Working smart means working in ways that wring the most value out of the two most important assets you have: your time, and your relationships with your customers. Much of that is accomplished by thinking — specifically, by planning and preparing.

By managing your time effectively, you pack more quality sales contacts into your day. By strategizing and preparing, you improve the quality of your interactions with your customers. It's an issue of both quality and quantity.

If you're able to improve both, you will improve in leaps and bounds. Put the two together, and you have a prescription for performance that surpasses the ordinary.

6. Continuous Self-Improvement. There was a time when we learned our job, and then didn't need to think about learning again. Unfortunately, that was before the world began to change so rapidly. With knowledge doubling every two years, we have to double our personal store of knowledge every two years just to keep up. And, as the pace of knowledge creation continues to speed up, you'll need to continually improve the pace at which you acquire information and transform it into a usable format.

Over time, learning is the ultimate skill. Given enough time, the salesperson who is better at learning will eventually surpass all the others. One of the things I counsel sales managers to look for in prospective salespeople is the "ability and propensity to learn." Mastering the ability to learn is the ultimate sales competency.

Beginning in the next chapter, we'll take an in-depth look at each of the six essential competencies. Master these skills, and you'll be successful beyond your greatest expectations.

To implement the ideas in this chapter...

Identify and analyze your strategic advantage by answering these questions:

1. What objective, economic value does your company bring to your customers, relative to:

   • Manufacturers who may sell direct?

   • Other distributors who compete directly with you?

   • Alternate forms of distribution, such as mail order companies and warehouse clubs?

2. Why should one of your customers buy from you, personally, rather than one of your competitors?

3. What is your strategic advantage in the market?

4. How can you turn that advantage into more business?

Chapter Three
Getting Organized —
Part One:
The Starting Point

Let's start by looking at your job as a salesperson in its most basic terms. If I asked you to describe your job in the most fundamental ways, I suspect you'd use words like selling, products, and dollars. You're not alone. Most salespeople think of themselves as sellers of product. That's one of the most common job-related paradigms.

You know what a paradigm is — it's a fundamental belief that colors our perspective. It shapes the way we see the world. To see our jobs as they are in the '90s, we need a paradigm change.

Let me suggest another way to look at your job. You don't sell products to people, you build relationships with people, influencing them to buy things. Working with people is the process you're involved in and the focus of your energy. Products and money are the elements that flow through the sales process. Their changing hands is the consequence of what you do. If you focus on the process of building relationships with people, and not the products, you'll be able to understand your job much more clearly.

Here's a helpful concept to enable you to shift your paradigm.

Let's start with your annual sales goals. Look at Illustration # 3. It's a work sheet that you can use to work through this first concept. Begin by asking yourself the question, "How much do I want to sell this year?" What? You don't have a goal? Shame on you. The first step in selling is to decide how much you want to sell. Setting a goal energizes you, focuses you, and makes it easy for you to develop strategy. So, before you do anything else, develop an annual sales goal.

Here's a good, workable way to arrive at an annual sales goal. First, look at last year's sales, account by account, and determine what you think you can sell this year in each account. Then add up those figures. Next add in the number you think you can sell to new accounts. The sum of these two numbers is your annual sales goal.

Once you have an annual sales goal, write it down on a form that looks like Illustration # 3. In the example, I'm going to set a goal of $1,000,000 in sales.

Now, let's translate this dollar goal into people goals. As long as you concentrate on selling *things*, you won't reach your sales potential. You need to express your goals in terms of *people*, not money.

Think in terms of two different kinds of sales tasks: acquiring new customers, and expanding the business with current customers. Think about your annual goal, and split it into two parts. On the left, indicate how much of that goal will come from new customers, and how much from current customers. It is possible that you may have 100 percent of your goal in one category or the other, but most salespeople will have some in each side.

In my example, I'm going to suggest that $ 1/4 million will come from new customers, and $ 3/4 million will come from current customers. Break your numbers into those two categories.

Salesperson: _____

Segment: _____

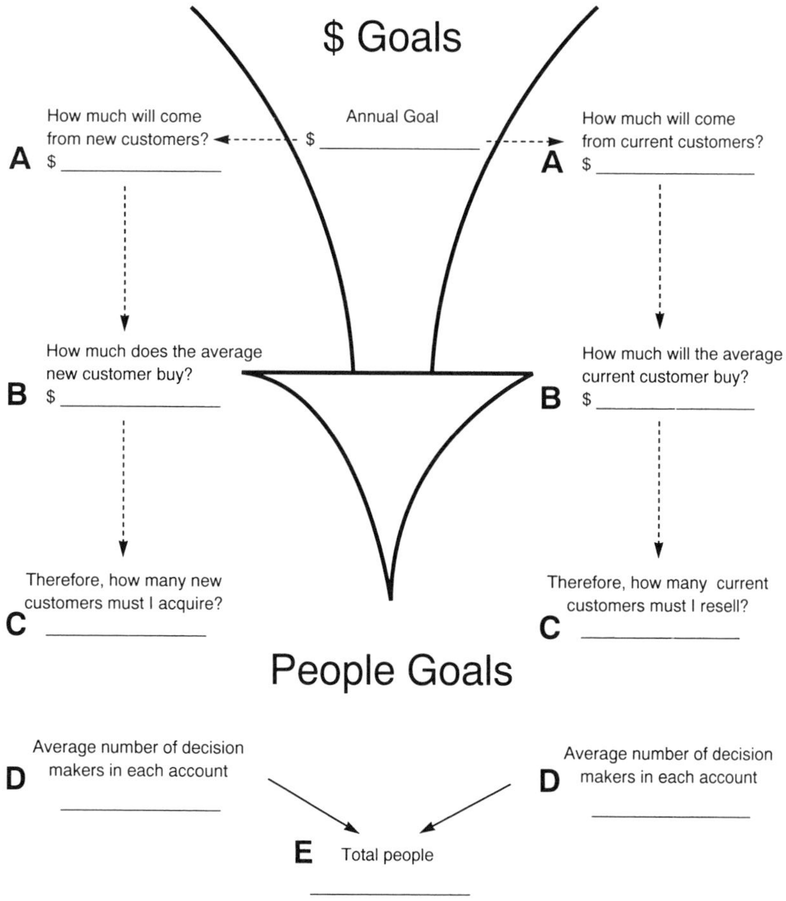

$ Goals

How much will come
from new customers? ◄------ $ _____ ------► How much will come
from current customers?

A $ _____   Annual Goal   **A** $ _____

How much does the average
new customer buy?

B $ _____

How much will the average
current customer buy?

B $ _____

Therefore, how many new
customers must I acquire?

C _____

Therefore, how many current
customers must I resell?

C _____

People Goals

Average number of decision
makers in each account

D _____

Average number of decision
makers in each account

D _____

E Total people

_____

Illustration #3

Now, estimate what an average new customer buys from you in the course of the first year. Let's say $50,000. What does your average current customer buy from you in the course of a year? Let's say $75,000. Think of your own territory/situation right now, and write down the average on the appropriate lines. Now, divide the total (line A) by the average (line B). Write down the answer on line C.

That number reflects the number of accounts you must deal with successfully. Add in one more factor. This time, estimate the number of decision makers and influencers you must positively relate to in the average account. Write it down on line D. Now, multiply the number of accounts by this number and write the answer on line E.

This represents the total number of people you must successfully influence if you want to reach your goals.

I call this number your *people goals.* You began with dollar goals, and translated them into people goals. Now you know exactly what your job is. You must influence a certain number of people to purchase from you for the first time, and a certain number to continue to buy from you.

You're now focused on the people aspect of your job. And that's an important first step to getting organized.

Understanding Your Job Description

Now, let's look at your job description from this new perspective of "people influencing." Look at illustration #4. Notice the area on the far left. I like to call that area *the land of total apathy and complete ignorance.* That's where your potential customers live. They don't know you exist and they don't care. They are totally ignorant of you, and totally apathetic.

Your job as a salesperson is to pluck them out of the land of apathy and ignorance, and to form a relationship with them

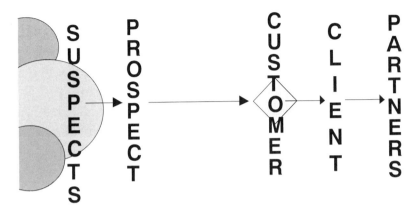

Illustration #4

that leads them to trust you to the point that they give you a competitive edge over everyone else.

The first step in the process is for you to examine the world of apathy and ignorance and identify some suspects. What is a suspect? Someone you suspect might use your product.

The next step is to put them through a process to screen some out and screen some in. You start with a large quantity of suspects and end up with a smaller quantity of prospects.

What's a prospect? Someone who has a definite need or interest in what you are selling, someone who can make the decision, and, someone who can pay for it. It's no use wasting your time with people who are non-prospects. The process of turning suspects into prospects is an essential step of the procedure. It generally requires you to ask questions, do some research, and then make some decisions about the individual with whom you are speaking.

Having sifted through the world of suspects and identified some prospects, the next step in your job is to turn those prospects into customers.

What is a customer? Someone who buys. They give you money in exchange for what you have to offer. That's a major shift in the relationship. You now are on totally different ground. You're on their vendor list. Your name is in their computer files. And, they trust you enough to buy something from you. You've taken a major step forward in the relationship.

Now, your task is to turn customers into clients. What is a client? Someone who buys regularly. This is a critical step in the process. Generally, you haven't made any real money on the customers yet because the cost in time and energy of bringing them from suspects to customers is very high relative to the amount of return you receive on the initial order. To make that investment pay off, you need to invest more energy and time in influencing them to buy again and again. When you do, you've created a client.

Finally, you need to turn clients into partners. What are partners? Customers who buy everything they can from you, who are really close to you and dependent on you. Customers who are so pleased with you, your products, and your services that they tell other people about you. Customers who rely on you, and see you and your company as an integral part of their businesses.

When you begin to think about relationship building with your customers and your prospects, it helps to think about it as a progression. The relationship progresses from mutual suspicion, step by step, until it reaches mutual respect, admiration and interdependence.

It is just like a romantic relationship. You start out with someone you don't know but to whom you are somewhat attracted. The relationship builds because of communication and sharing. The relationship grows deeper as each side takes risks.

Good distributor salespeople take people from being suspects and create involvement with them until they become partners with them and their companies.

Life is a lot easier when you have a bunch of customers as partners. That is where you make most of your money, enjoy the most satisfying relationships, and develop the most creative solutions. It's also where you are the most productive. Your sales per account will be higher, and your margins will be higher, because you won't have the same level of competition.

So, if you're going to excel at distributor sales, you need to focus on moving people closer and closer into a relationship with you. The ultimate result of your selling efforts is a number of accounts who are "partners," and a number of others who are steadily moving in that direction.

Here's an exercise to help you personalize this concept. Create a list of all the people you interact with in your market. Next to each name, rank that person as a suspect, prospect, client, customer, or champion.

Now, let me challenge you to apply this concept to another group of people — manufacturer's reps. That's right, those scumball, two-faced, back-biting incompetents you're forced to tolerate. Just suppose you could create relationships with them such that they want to work with you exclusively, they direct business your way, and they actually help you sell their products. If that were the case, that rep would be a "partner" also.

You could apply this organizational scheme to each of the reps who is active in your territory. In other words, a suspect would be a rep who might enter into a positive business relationship with you. A prospect would be one who could really work with you, is accessible, and willing to talk with you. A customer would be a rep who actually does work with you. A client would be one who works with you regularly, and a partner would be a rep who works with you exclusively, likes you, and can be counted on to send you business.

As a distributor salesperson you must understand that manufacturer's reps are your customers too. If you can bring them into relationships with you, you can get them working for you.

One of the most successful things for me was working systematically with manufacturer's reps. I had one rep in particular who stood out. As I was organizing myself, I looked analytically at all the lines my company carried, and identified the lines that had the potential to bring me the biggest dollar return. I looked at the reps who handled those lines, and identified one who appeared to be a high-potential "prospect."

She was the strongest rep for my highest-potential company. Fortunately, she saw me the same way. So, together, we built a strong relationship that made us both a lot of money. Over four years, she became the number one salesperson in the nation for that company, and I became the number one salesperson for my company. One of my proudest accomplishments was the letter of recommendation I received from her boss, noting that I was the number one distributor rep in the nation for that manufacturer. More business went through me than any other distributor rep in the country. That was a direct result of applying this mind set to the issue of manufacturers reps.

To personalize this concept, repeat the exercise I talked about above, this time listing each of your manufacturer's reps instead of each of your customers. Then categorize them, identifying each as a suspect, prospect, customer, client, or partner.

This is an excellent exercise to help you focus on the most important parts of your job. As you begin to think this way, you'll see that your job is to take everyone to the next step. All the suspects in the world need to be turned into prospects.

Appropriate prospects need to be turned into customers. Customers need to be matured into clients, and clients into partners. What do you do with partners? Keep them! Do whatever it takes. They're the ones who pay your bills.

ABC prospects and customers

Now that you've got an idea of what your job description is, let's extend this idea of organizing yourself by prioritizing where you should spend your time most effectively. Some prospects and customers have more potential than others. If you're going to excel at distributor sales, you need to work as intelligently as you can. That means spending time in the most effective ways. "ABC Analysis" will tell you where to spend your time.

The concept is that some prospects and customers have more potential than others. You should spend the most time with those who offer the highest potential.

Think about the idea of "high potential." I define high potential as offering the opportunity of maximum dollars returned on the minimum time invested. You may be thinking that this sounds like common sense, and it is. The problem is that most distributor salespeople don't exercise the discipline of applying that common sense. Instead, they do two other things.

First, they go through the motions of being active. In other words, they keep busy calling on whoever will see them, rather than focusing on those people who hold the greatest potential. Instead of going where it's smart, they go where it's comfortable and routine.

The second mistake distributor salespeople often make is assuming that history equals potential. In truth, history has nothing to do with potential. In other words, just because an account has been a good customer in the past, doesn't mean that it is a high potential customer for the future.

Now, let's take this concept one level deeper. What constitutes "high potential?"

I like to think that potential is comprised of two components. The first is *quantified potential.* That refers to the amount of your product they can buy. Obviously each account has a potential to purchase differing amounts of your product. When you objectively measure the size of that need, you have quantified the potential.

But that's only half of the issue. The second component relates directly to the earlier discussion of suspects and partners. Which of your accounts rank high in potential *partnerability? Partnerability* is that subjective feeling you gain about the account's potential to eventually become a partner. How is the chemistry between the two companies, and between yourself and your contact people? Is the account just a price buyer, or is it open to creative proposals from you? Is it a progressive, growing organization? Those are some of the issues that comprise *partnerability.* You may have one account that has huge quantifiable potential, but because of their philosophy or the personalities of the decision makers, no foreseeable *partnerability.* That account would not be a high-potential account.

Let's say you have a very large account that offers tremendous potential. At the same time, you know the business is very competitive, that every other distributor is working to penetrate that account. This account has long used one of your competitors and he appears to be very solid in the account. This account ranks low in potential partnerability. A sober assessment means that you'll have to invest countless hours, maybe years, before you can have any realistic opportunity to sell anything.

On the other hand, what if you have a much smaller account in which you have a realistic possibility of closing some business after just a couple calls? Which one would rank higher on the "potential for time invested" scale? Obviously, the second does.

That's the kind of hard-nosed analysis that helps you to get organized for more effective selling.

Let's take that concept now, and apply it to two different groups of people; your prospects, and your customers. On a sheet of paper, create three columns. The first is the "A" column into which you're going to place those prospects and customers who are in the top 10 to 30 percent of all your prospects and customers. So, if you have 20 total prospects, you should identify 2 to 6 as "A" prospects. Remember, these represent the highest potential dollars returned for time invested. Focus on the future.

Then, cull out those who appear to offer a limited return on time invested. Take somewhere between 10 to 60 percent and put them in the "C" column. Those are your lowest priority prospects and customers.

Finally, put all those who are left over in the "B" column. They represent the middle group of prospects and customers.

You can do this exercise on two levels. At the first level, rank all your *accounts* and *prospective accounts* according to this ABC criteria. At the second level, rank all the *individuals* within those accounts by this criteria. In other words, you may have 12 people who are potential decision makers or influences within a particular "A" account. Who represents the highest potential? Who the least?

When you've done that, you've organized the most important aspect of your job — your customers and prospects.

To implement the ideas in this chapter...

1. Create an annual sales goal for this year, and translate it into people goals.

2. Categorize all of your accounts using the suspects, prospects, customers, clients, partners system.

3. Do the same with all the individuals within your accounts.

4. Do the same with all the manufacturer's reps within your territory.

5. Create a definition of "partnerability" that fits your industry.

6. Sort all of your prospects into ABC categories.

7. Sort all of your customers into ABC categories.

8. Sort all of the individual contact people within your accounts into ABC categories.

Chapter Four
Organizing Yourself — Part Two: Managing Information

One of the most troublesome areas for distributor salespeople is that of organizing information. It's tempting to fall into the trap of spending hours reviewing information, and it's easy to become overwhelmed by it. Think of the number of manufacturers you represent. Multiply that by the number of new products they introduce each year, then by the number of price increases and product updates. Next, add in the constantly changing requirements and expectations of your customers. Multiply that by the number of your competitors and all the products they sell. Finally, factor in your competitors' changes in strategy and personnel.

Beginning to get the picture? That's all information you must deal with. If you're not careful, you can spend all your time looking at computer screens and reading mail.

To be effective as a distributor salesperson, you need to manage your information. That means that you must create systems to collect the information that will be most useful to you, and then keep it readily available. Since our world is constantly producing new information, your system isn't the kind of thing you do once and forget. Rather, it has to be a dynamic system that enables you to process, sort, store and access new information continuously.

Creating and maintaining your system is a matter of following several specific steps.

To begin, list the kinds of information you think will be most useful to you. Think about your job and determine what kinds of information you'd like to have to help you deal effectively with your customers. Here's a partial list that would fit most distributor reps:

- Information about your customers and prospects.

- Information about the manufacturers you represent and their products.

- Information about your competitors.

- Information about the manufacturer's reps you work with.

- Information about your company's programs and promotions.

Add to this list anything else you think is important. For example, if you're in a highly-technical area, you may want to collect information about technological innovations or applications.

Now that you've gotten your list together, think about the information in each category that would be *ideal* for you to have.

Start at the top and work down. Look at customers and prospects first. What, ideally, would you like to know about them? I'd suggest, at a minimum, that you need to have an account profile form for each individual decision maker as well as one for each account.

You're probably wondering, "What's an account profile form?" Glad you asked.

Account Profile Form

An account profile form is a form full of questions, or more precisely, spaces for the answers to questions. The questions are all about one of your accounts, or one of the individuals within that account. The form is the document on which you store that useful information.

A well-designed, systematically executed account profile form can be one of your most powerful strategies for acquiring a competitive edge.

Here's why. First, it provides you a way to collect quantitative information that will allow you to know your customers more thoroughly than your competition. For example, you can have spaces for information about the account's total volume of the kind of products you sell, the dates of contracts that are coming up, the people from whom they are currently buying, and so forth. All of that seems pretty basic. However, most salespeople have no systematic way of collecting and storing that information. So, while you may occasionally ask a certain customer for parts of it, you probably aren't asking every customer for all the information. And, you're probably not collecting it, storing it, and referring to it in a systematic, disciplined way.

For example, do you think your competitors know exactly how much potential each of their accounts has? Do you think they know how many pieces of production equipment each customer has, and the manufacturer and year of purchase of each? Probably not.

If you collect good quantitative marketing information, you'll be better equipped to make strategic sales decisions. For example, you'll know exactly who to talk to when the new piece of equipment from ABC manufacturer is finally introduced. And, you'll know who is really ripe for some new cost-saving product that's coming, or that new program your company is putting together.

In addition to the quantitative information, the form provides a system for collecting personal information about the key decision makers. Once you have a place for "hobbies" and "organizations belonged to" you'll have to collect that information and fill in the space. Now, imagine getting ready for the next sales call on that customer and reviewing the things that he likes to talk about, refreshing your memory on the name of his spouse, and the names and schools of each of the kids.

Do you think you'll be better prepared to have an enjoyable, relationship-building conversation with that customer than your competitor will? Of course you will.

The act of asking the questions prompted by the form also creates a process of deeper communication between you and your customer. You'll talk about deeper things and more personal things than most of your competitors. Your customer perceives your inquiries as sincere interest (which they are) and responds to you accordingly.

Finally, the form allows you to store important information someplace other than in your head. The problem with keeping information only in your head is that it isn't always readily accessible. When you want to have a relaxed conversation with one of your customers about his interests, you can't always remember that he golfs and was a starting halfback on his college football team. However, if you have that information stored on a form, you can review it just before you go in to see your customer, and put it foremost in your mind.

To some degree, every good salesperson implements these concepts. The difference between the run-of-the-mill salesperson and the master, however, is the degree to which the master disciplines himself to stick to a systematic approach. Most salespeople do it as they think of it, but don't keep the information systematically. Masters understand the need to discipline themselves, and thus do a more thorough job of collecting information.

Have I sold you on the need to use an account profile form? Good. As you begin to implement this idea, think in terms of two types of forms. The first captures the account-information — size, number of employees, etc. The second focuses on the individual decision makers within that account, and contains personal information — like hobbies, outside interests, etc. You should have one account form for every account, and as many personal profiles as there are key contact people within that account.

Here's how to design and implement this idea.

1. Identify each of the markets you sell to. You may sell to a number of different kinds of customers. Each different type of business should have it's own version of the form. For example, I sold to hospitals, large outpatient clinics, and independent laboratories. The differences between these institutions were enormous, and each had a different business structure, set of needs, and decision-making apparatus. So each warranted a unique account profile form.

2. Create a list. Begin the form by first listing all of the things you'd like to know about your account. For example, you might find it useful to know the number of employees, the SIC code, which competitors are currently involved in the account, and so on. The key is to determine the information that is *useful* to you.

Then, list all of the things you'd like to know about each individual decision maker, influencer, or gatekeeper within that account. This is generally personal information such as where they went to school, their interests and hobbies, people who you both may know, the organizations they belong to, and other similar information.

If you have small accounts with only one major decision maker, one version of the form will be enough. It will contain both account information, as well as personal information.

However, if you sell to larger institutions with a number of departments or decision makers, then you'll want to have one version of the form for the account itself, and another for the individual information. You may end up with one document for the company and 10 to 15 individual profiles for all the key people within that account.

Take several days to complete an exhaustive list, writing down ideas as they come to you.

3. Edit. Now, edit your list of ideas down to those pieces of information you consider most useful. You probably can't collect everything, so collect the information that is most useful. Start with the basics — name, title, and so on, and add the important business information like how much of each of your product categories that account purchases each year, what kind of business it is, and what the reporting relationships and decision-making processes are.

4. Design the form. Now, create the form with spaces for each of the answers to the questions you listed above.

Don't get too involved in creating the perfect looking document. No matter how thorough a job you've done, you'll probably revise the form in a few weeks after you have some experience working with it. So, design something that is workable for now, and let your day-to-day use create the fine-tuning adjustments that you'll make along the way.

5. Implement. Begin to use the form to collect information on every sales call. This doesn't mean that you set down with pen in hand and interrogate every customer, although a little of that is appropriate.

Rather, review the form before each sales call, solidifying in your mind the information you already have and determining what you need. Then, in the course of the conversation, attempt to listen specifically for those pieces of information that you're still lacking. Completing the form may take six months of sales calls.

6. Refine. Review your master form from time to time and revise it as you get experience with it. You'll soon determine what information is impossible to collect, and what really isn't useful.

7. Refer to it. Store your forms in a place that you can access each time you call on that account. I suggest you create an account folder for each customer, and that you keep your forms there. Refer to them before every sales call. By reading over the personal information you've stored on the form, you'll find it fresh in your mind, and you'll be much more likely to work it into a conversation. All of your efforts to create the form and collect information will be wasted if you don't use it before every sales call.

Next, refer to the account information when you're doing your strategic planning, when you're deciding who are your "A," "B," and "C" accounts, and when you're thinking about where to present some new program or product line.

Contact Log

The next information collection and storage tool is a contact log. It's just a simple record of what you talked about in each visit, and what your plan is at that point. It sounds simple, and it is.

But again, most people don't discipline themselves to systematically collect and store this information. Instead, they rely on their memory. I don't know about you, but I know that if I make several sales calls during the course of a day, by the end of the day, I've forgotten half of everything I talked about. If I don't write it down, immediately after the call, I'll lose it. The same is probably true for you.

The contact log can take several forms. I preferred to use 3" X 5" cards. They were small and inconspicuous, they could be easily kept in my breast pocket wallet or planner, and they were readily available. After each call, I'd simply write down what happened, and what I needed to do next. When a card was filled up, I'd number it and file it in the account folder. That way, I could review years worth of sales calls to see the history of a contract or piece of business.

If you prefer, use a legal pad or simple 8 1/2" by 11" lined pages.

Finally, with today's technology, you can use a laptop computer and contact management software to collect and store the same information.

Regardless of the technology you decide to use, the important thing is that you make a systematic and disciplined effort to record your contacts.

Account Files

One last information management tool to help you with your prospects and customers is your account files. Create a set of manila folders or pocket files for each of our accounts. You'll probably need at least two files for each account. In one, keep all historically important information. For example, keep copies of all the quotes you've made to that account and, on each, note who got the business, when it may come up again, and your best understanding of why someone else was awarded the business. Any other notes that you've made regarding competitors, or other helpful information about the account, should go into the historical file.

The other file is your working file. This is the one you take with you to the account. Keep your profiles, contact logs, and current quotes and proposals in there. You may also use it to carry pieces of literature you intend to leave with your account, as well as any helpful pieces of information that you may need while you're on the sales call.

When you have this filing system in place, you've organized the most important part of your job — the information about your customers and prospects. Now it's time to organize the information needed in the other aspects of your job.

To implement the ideas in this chapter...

1. List the kinds of information you think will be most useful to you.

2. Concentrate on each item on your list, and describe the ideal information you'd like to have in that category.

3. Create an account profile form.

4. Create a personal profile form.

5. Begin to systematically use the two forms to collect useful marketing information.

6. Create a contact log form.

7. Begin to use it for every customer contact.

8. Create a set of account files for each of your customers.

Chapter Five
Getting Organized –
Part Three:
Files, Files, & More Files

Now that you've got the most critical portion of your job organized, you need to tackle some other important areas of information management.

Competitor Files

Set up manila folders for each of your main competitors. If your territory overlaps with several reps from the same competitor, you may need to have a folder for each of those reps.

Then, anytime you collect a piece of information about a competitor, put it in the appropriate file. When you lose a piece of business to a competitor, note what products were lost, when and by how much. When you see some evidence of that competitor promoting a certain product line to one of your accounts, store that information. In time, you'll have collected a powerful bank of useful information.

Refer to it regularly. You'll find it particularly helpful in a big, competitive bid when you're trying to figure out what everyone else is going to do.

Tickler Files

A tickler file is just a convenient way to jog your memory when there is something you need to do. Here's an easy way to set one up. Get a file that holds 3" X 5" cards, and set up indexes with labels for every month from January through December, and another set with labels numbered 1 through 31.

Then, when you want to be reminded to do something, write it on a 3" X 5" card, and put it under the appropriate month you need to be reminded to take action. Let's say you present a new product line to one of your accounts. Your contact says that it's currently under contract, but he'd be willing to consider an evaluation of your product line in June. Simply put a little note to talk to that account about the new product line on a 3" X 5" card, and file it in the June section.

Then, on the first of June, take every card out of the June file, and place it in the number file that corresponds to the date that you want to talk to your account about it. Do this with every card in the monthly section every month. Then, each day, review the things you need to do that day. It's a simple way to keep organized and make sure that nothing slips through the cracks.

If you're using a computer, contact management software can substitute for this tickler file.

Product Files

You need to keep information about the products you sell as well as the manufacturers you represent. Some of you are thinking, "I don't need to have that, it's all at the office." The problem with that is that you must go to the office to get it. And every time you go to the office you waste precious selling time.

I recommend that you keep a separate, duplicate set of files at your home. These files should contain two sets of information. The first file is a reference file with technical details, competitor's products, and so on, that you may need to study from time to time. Include in it the names of the manufacturers, their sales managers, product managers, and the home office 800 numbers.

The second file should contain the literature that you'll need to hand out.

Manufacturer Rep Files

A manufacturer's rep can be one of your greatest assets. Winning one over to work with you can be one of the smartest strategies you can undertake.

If you have reps who are on your side and working in your territory, it's like multiplying yourself. They can create interest in their product and help direct the business your way. Every time they do that, it saves you time and multiplies your effectiveness.

But converting a manufacturer's rep takes work, just like winning over a customer does. Begin by thinking of each manufacturer's rep as a potential customer to be won over. Approach the task in the same way you would sell a new customer.

This means creating a set of files on each of the manufacturer's reps who are active in your territory. Develop a personal profile for each one in the same way that you developed a profile for each of the decision makers in your accounts.

I used 5" X 7" cards for each one, with profiles at the top of each card, and a contact log below and on the back of the card. Every time I talked to a rep, or worked with one of them, I'd note it on the contact log. Nothing escaped with that system.

Other Files

1. Internal communications. From time to time you'll need to create, process or keep paperwork for someone inside your business. Create a couple of files for that eventuality – perhaps one for customer service, another for purchasing or inventory control, a final one for your boss.

2. General learning. The need to continue to improve in your job means that you'll need to dedicate time to the task of learning. When you see a good article about sales skills, relationship building, or perhaps some aspect of an application of your products, put it into your learning file, and review it when you set time aside to do so.

Information Management

When you have completed the organization of your file system, you've created most of the tools you need to implement an information management system.

Creating and effectively using such a system is one of the marks of a master distribution salesperson. Our information-rich age brings with it a strong temptation to wallow in information. Without a system to manage information, information will manage you.

You can review manufacturer's product literature for hours every day. You can study last week's sales reports and credit memos, review the details of a manufacturer's sales promotion, revisit the last ten sales calls you made to an account, all while you channel surf around 40 TV stations or cruise the Internet.

The trick is to create a system that allows you to handle the flood of information, and then to operate the system with discipline. The quicker you handle information, the more hours you'll have to devote to selling.

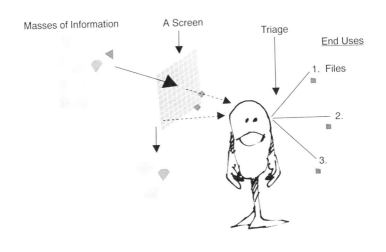

Illustration #5

Look at Illustration # 5. It illustrates the processing involved in creating your system. The first element you need is a *screen* to eliminate information that isn't worth your time. Next, you need a set of *criteria* on which to triage that information. Finally, you need some *destinations* to file the information.

Let's look at how this works.

1. Screening. In today's world, the issue isn't so much acquiring good information as it is screening out useless, time-wasting information. The way you do that is to develop criteria for what is worth looking at, and what isn't. These criteria should be turned into a couple of simple questions you ask yourself about each tempting morsel of information that comes your way.

For example, you might say, "I won't look at anything that isn't directly related to my job as a salesperson." Then, you sit down to watch TV and see the governor talking about a new tax plan. You ask yourself, "Is this directly related to my job as a salesperson?" If the answer is "No," then click the remote again. If the answer is "Yes," then stay right there and take in the information.

2. Triaging. Next, you need to create the habit of "triaging" information. Perhaps you've seen triage areas in hospital emergency rooms. It's the area where a new patient is taken to allow someone to make a quick assessment of his or her condition. The patient is then directed to one of a number of different areas depending on his or her condition. Some patients will be sent immediately to the operating room, others will be asked to wait longer, some will be transported to the morgue. The triage process is one of quickly assessing and then directing the subject into any one of a number of different destinations depending on the results of the assessment.

You should do the same thing with information. Quickly assess where this piece of information should be stored or processed, and then put it there. Your destinations are the files you have created. For example, let's say you arrive at the office and review the contents of your mail box. Among other things, you find a memo from your manager outlining the details of a new procedure for placing orders electronically. You ask yourself a screening question, "Does this directly affect my job?" In this case, the answer is "No" because you don't place orders electronically. The memo goes into the wastebasket.

The next several items are new product releases from some of your manufacturers. You ask yourself the screening question, and the answer is "Yes." You then decide, by triaging, how you can use that information and where it should be sent. In this case, you put two of the product releases on one pile, and stick a post-it note on it with the words "product file." You don't think you'll have much use for them, but you want them in the product files where you can access them if you need to. The other five product categories appear to have some potential, so you paper clip them together with a post-it that says "learning file."

Finally, you received a printout of the credit memos issued in your territory. You take a quick look at it, see that there's nothing particularly revealing in it, and decide to file that in the round file on the floor next to the desk.

With that, you've processed the batch of information by first screening and then triaging everything into one of the destinations you previously created.

That's how you create your system to process information and control the amount of time you spend handling it. The only missing link is your discipline to do it.

Once you've set up the system, and developed the principles and procedures to make it work, it's up to you to relentlessly apply it. If you do, you'll save countless hours which you can devote to the productive parts of your job. Your disciplined use of the system will keep you from wasting hundreds of hours wallowing in information that isn't useful to you.

To implement the ideas in this chapter...

1. Create a set of competitor files.

2. Develop a tickler file and begin to use it.

3. Create a set of product files.

4. Create a set of files for your manufacturer reps.

5. Create a set of files for your internal communications.

6. Create your general learning files.

7. Write up a set of criteria for screening incoming information.

8. Begin to use the screening and triaging processes discussed in this chapter.

Chapter Six
Relationship Building – Part One: Eight Powerful Rules

Distributor sales reps, more than any other type, must be good at relationship building.

That's because you see your customers more often, and for longer periods of time than almost any other type of salesperson. To be successful in your job, you must build relationships that help you wear well with your customers. If you're very good at it, your relationships can provide you a competitive edge over all of your competitors.

Imagine this. You walk into a standing appointment with one of your largest customers. The receptionist greets you by your first name, and asks about your family. The main decision maker calls you right in, while one of your competitors sits in the waiting room. You visit together for about an hour, during which time he shares some information about new items coming up on the budget, and suggests you see one of the department managers who is having a problem.

You discuss a new product line your company recently acquired, and he indicates that the prospects are good for them to use it. He suggests price levels which would make your new product line attractive to the account.

While you're in his office, he calls and makes two appointments for you – one with the department head, and the other with the main decision maker for the new product line.

You decide to go to lunch together. As you walk out, you see the competitor salesperson is gone. Over lunch, you don't mention business, but instead talk about personal things. You genuinely enjoy each other's company.

That's what the fruits of powerful relationship building look like.

Your skillful relationship building has earned your customer's *comfortable preference.* That's your competitive edge. With everything else being equal, you get the business. In a world where the distinctions between your company and your competitors are growing less and less clear to your customer, your relationship may be your only real competitive edge.

Often, the only reason a piece of business goes to one salesperson or the other is the depth and length of the personal relationship. Your customer likes you, so you get the business. Relationship building, then, is a key competency for success in the '90s.

Your most powerful strategy is to make yourself important to your customers. What does that mean? It means you must become a difficult-to-replace, integral part of your customer's business and his job. Doing so makes you valuable to your manufacturers as well as to your customers.

When it comes down to basic values, do you know what a manufacturer really wants from you?

It doesn't matter how efficient your distribution systems are, nor how powerful your computers. Those are nice, but from the manufacturer's perspective, they're icing on the cake. What they really want from you is access to the customer. If you are important to your customers, you provide more access to them than your competitor. And that's called job security.

The more important you are to your customers, the more important you are to your manufacturers. You operate as an extremely effective interface between the two.

In order to <u>earn</u> this important position, you will have to implement the following eight rules for relationship building.

Eight Rules for Relationship Building

1. Give first. Remember the law of reciprocity? It may be one of the single most powerful laws that governs human behavior for salespeople. The law simply states that people will act toward you the way you first act toward them. If you want good information and honesty from them, what do you have to do first? The law of reciprocity dictates that you must share important information and be honest with them first.

In every meeting with a customer, try to bring him something of value. It can be an idea, like what someone else is doing with a product or service you offer. It can be a story about a new product, or a new program. It can be something you read in an industry journal, or a clipping from a trade journal that has an idea your customer can use. The important thing is to try, at every meeting, to bring something of value.

As you consistently do this, a couple of things will happen. First, your customers begin to see you as someone other than "just a salesperson." Rather, they see you as a valuable associate, someone who really understands their business and has their best interests in mind.

Next, they begin to look forward to your visits, knowing that you'll bring something of value with you. After a while, they'll take your calls graciously, and try to make time to see you.

Also, when you give first, it creates a subconscious debt on their part. After a while, they feel like they have to return the gift with a piece of business or competitive information from which you can benefit.

This rule has a corollary. If you're always committed to giving first, it implies that, if you don't have something of value to bring, you won't attempt to see your customers. Never take up their valuable time unless you have a legitimate, valuable item (valuable from their perspective, not from yours) to discuss.

Respect for your customers' time gradually creates a respect for yours in them. After a while, they'll see you every time you ask because they know that you have something of value to discuss. Your reputation precedes you – and that's a reputation you have consciously built with discipline and forethought.

2. Avoid failure. Simple enough. But like most of the simplest, most basic rules, we often violate it.

My father was a salesperson. Interestingly, he was a salesperson for a distributor. I remember, as a child, spending the day with him. I was 8 or 10, and it was my first taste of distributor sales. I clearly remember talking to him after one of his sales calls. He said, "Your enemies don't buy from you."

What a simple observation. But what profound implications. Of course! Your enemies don't buy from you. So, whatever you do, avoid making enemies. Do just the opposite – make friends instead.

Making enemies is failure. You make enemies, and fail, by destroying the relationship. Don't get thrown out. Don't aggravate people to the point where you make them an enemy. Don't be so strong and so pushy that you make an enemy. Enemies won't buy from you. Avoid failure.

I learned about avoiding failure by failing. At one point in my career, I sold surgical staplers. At the time, this was a new concept for surgeons, and it had to be sold in a novel way. Our first task was to sell ourselves into the hospital operating room suite, and then into the surgeons' lounge. There, we changed out of our street clothes and into surgeon's greens. We hung around the surgeons' lounge, drinking coffee and waiting for the right surgeons to come in. When one would come in to change clothes to get ready for surgery, we would approach him and demonstrate the staplers. Then we'd say "Now doctor, if you would like to try this, I'd be happy to scrub your next case with you."

And we did. We took part on the surgical team, standing right next to the surgeon – gowned and gloved and "scrubbed" like the others. At that point, we had an opportunity to sell our equipment.

My lesson came when I was a little too strong in one hospital. The Chief of Surgery said to the OR supervisor, "Get him out of here." I left and was not welcome back because I made an enemy. I failed.

I learned that I must keep the door open no matter what. The long-term relationship is always more important than the short-term sale. No single deal is worth jeopardizing the relationship.

3. Develop trust. See people only when you have something worthwhile to see them about.

Distributor salespeople often get caught up in the activity and the regularity of sales calls. In other words, you may spend much of your time going through the motions, out of habit. For example, you may see a certain customer every Tuesday at 10:00 A.M., not because it's smart, but because it's habit. The temptation is to mindlessly go through the motions.

To overcome this tendency, *have a reason* to see each person each time. Make sure you have something worthwhile to talk to them about. If you don't, then don't see them. Bring something worthwhile every time so you build up trust. They know you will not waste their time. And, time is the commodity of the '90s. It's the most important thing your customer has. Respect their time, and they'll respect you.

4. Reduce the risk of every decision. The biggest issue in the minds of your customers and prospects is *risk*. Whenever you present them with a decision to make, the biggest thing they're thinking about, subconsciously, is risk. It's not just the money, it's the social, psychological and emotional cost that is also at risk.

In order to see this issue from your customers' perspective, you need to calculate the amount of risk that you expect your customers to accept when you offer them an opportunity to say "yes" to you. You can then work to reduce that risk. The lower the risk of the decision, the more likely your customer will say "yes."

Here's an illustration to help you understand this concept. Imagine that you are under orders by your spouse to pick up a package of disposable cups on the way home from work today because you're having friends over for dessert and drinks tonight. You stop at the local grocery store, and make a selection between brand A and brand B. You pick brand A.

When you bring the cups home, your spouse mixes up a pitcher of margaritas and pours one. The drink leaks out of the bottom of the cup and puddles on the counter. There is a hole in the bottom of the cup. You pour your drink into another cup and it leaks, too. In fact, every one of the cups *you bought* is defective.

What happens to you in this instant in time? What is the consequence of your decision? I don't know about you, but I would be the recipient of some negative emotion. That may be the most painful cost of your decision. But there are other costs. You're going to have to fix the problem. If there's time, you'll have to run back to the store and replace the cups. So, in addition to the emotional cost, you must pay in terms of extra time and additional money. All because of your bad decision. You accepted that risk when you made your decision.

Here's a simple exercise to help you understand this concept. Draw a short vertical line. At the top of the line write the number 25. At the bottom, write the number zero. Now on a scale of 0 - 25, where would you put the risk of buying a package of disposable cups? Most people would respond that it's close to zero.

At the other end of the scale, I have an adoption agency as a client. When a young lady is in a crisis pregnancy, and she's making a decision whether or not to release her unborn child for adoption, how big a risk is that for her?

Most people say that it's a 25. It's a lifetime of consequences for at least four people. That's a very high risk. The point of this exercise is that when you ask your prospects to say yes to you, they are accepting some risk. Each decision you ask of them carries with it a different degree of risk.

Imagine a typical prospect. Then think of the typical offer or decision you ask of that person. Now, put yourself in his shoes, and see the situation through his eyes. On the 0 - 25 scale, how much risk does he accept when he says "yes" to you?

Here's an easy way of calculating it. Just ask yourself what happens to that individual if you, or your company, messes up.

If the risk to that person is high, then you need to work to reduce that risk. If you want to build relationships in the '90s, look at every time you offer something to your customer and ask, "How do I reduce the risk?"

The winners in the competitive game are people who provide the same product or service at less risk. Reducing risk is a strategy for building relationships. If your prospect sees you as the lowest-risk source, he becomes comfortable with you. The relationship develops on the basis of this issue of risk.

5) Be remembered favorably. Try to end every interaction with a customer on a positive note. And, that generally means some kind of an agreement. When you get into this mind set it's not difficult to come to agreement. For example, a customer may call with a backorder problem. You say you'll check it out and call back tomorrow. You ask, "Will that be OK?"

When he says "OK," you have reached an agreement and ended the interaction favorably. This constant positive ending is an important factor in building positive relationships.

Here's an example from my personal experience. I recently changed car insurance after 15 years with the same company. I made the decision on the basis of price. Although I was delighted with the service my previous supplier had provided, the difference in price finally became more than I could justify.

So I switched my business. Then I called my former agent and told her. In that conversation, she said she appreciated the reason I was switching and could certainly understand. She appreciated me as a customer and asked if there is ever anything she could ever do for me to please call. She then said if there was any way she could facilitate the transfer, please tell her how she could help. Finally, she said that if I ever had a question about insurance to feel free to call her.

You can imagine how I felt. I wish she would have reacted angrily, that way I wouldn't have felt so bad. But, instead, she ended the interaction favorably. Now I look for my new company to mess up so I can give her back the business. That's a great example of ending every exchange favorably.

6. Keep the relationship process moving forward. Remember the chart showing the progression from "Suspect" to "Prospect?" Not only does that model provide a neat way to think about your job, but it can also be a working set of objectives that govern every meeting you conduct with customers and prospects.

Your job, and your objective for every meeting, is to move people ever closer in a relationship with you. Once you set your mind on the objective of continually moving people closer and closer to you, you'll find countless ways to do it.

However, if you never crystallize that as a objective, your relationship building will be happenstance rather than directed.

7. Broaden the relationship to include your company. A good relationship with a customer is larger than just you. It's a relationship between companies as well as between people. It's important to have a personal relationship. But it's also important that the companies have a relationship, too.

Facilitate that broader relationship at every occasion. Whenever you can arrange it, bring your managers in to see your customers. And do the opposite also. Bring your customers to see your facilities. The broader the relationship, the stronger it is. The more your customers know you, your company, and the other employees within your company, the more comfortable they are with you, and the more likely they are to do business with you.

8. Operate with 100% integrity. In my first professional sales position, I learned a powerful lesson: complete honesty is not only morally right, it is good business.

People deal with people they trust. Complete honesty gives

people reason to trust you. Lie to a customer, and they'll likely never forget it.

But integrity means more than just honesty. Integrity for a salesperson means that you do what you say you're going to do. You don't make promises quickly, you never promise something you're not sure of, you never over- promise, and you continually under-promise.

If you under-promise, you're in the position of always being able to deliver more than what your customer expected. That's an extremely powerful long-term relationship building strategy.

Integrity means that you never knowingly recommend something to a customer that you know isn't right for him. Remember, the long-term relationship is always more important than the short-term gain from an individual deal.

Finally, integrity means that you never speak badly about anyone, including your lowliest competitor. It's a funny thing about judging someone – it always tells the person to whom you're speaking more about *you* than it does about the person who is the subject of your scrutiny. Talk badly about someone, and the person you're talking to wonders if you'll say the same thing about him when you're talking to someone else.

If you're going to build solid relationships with your customers, be someone who is worth their trust and their time. Integrity gives you that standing.

To implement the ideas in this chapter...

1. Think about each of your "A" accounts, and ask yourself how you can become more important to each.

2. Brainstorm some ways you can *give first*. Try to implement at least one item on the list every day.

3. Reflect on a time when you have jeopardized a customer relationship. What did you do to cause that situation? What lesson is there in that for the future?

4. Resolve not to see your customers unless you have something of value to discuss with them.

5. Every time you present a proposal or demonstrate a product, ask yourself how you can reduce the risk of that decision for your customer.

6. Resolve to end every interaction with an agreement.

7. Identify the key decision makers within your "A" accounts. Label each as a "suspect, prospect, customer, client or partner." Then, think about each, and identify the things that have to happen to move each to the next category.

8. Resolve to bring some of the decision-makers from one of your "A" accounts into your facility at least once a month.

Chapter Seven
Relationship Building —
Part Two:
Reflective Behavior

If I asked you which animal good salespeople are most like, what would you say? Some people think immediately of a lion, roaring through the jungle — master of all he sees. Others say a fox, crafty and thoughtful. Still others say a dog, thinking of a dog's loyalty and friendliness.

None of these are my model. I like to think of good salespeople as being like chameleons. You're probably familiar with the chameleon. It's the lizard blessed with the unique ability to change colors to blend into its environment. If a chameleon is walking through green grass, it's green. If its running across brown sand, its brown.

Great salespeople have a similar ability. They reflect the behavioral style of their prospects and customers. Like the chameleon, they can "change colors" depending on the demands of the environment they find themselves in. I call this skill "reflective behavior." It's one of the most sophisticated and powerful relationship-building skills around.

As a professional salesperson intent on building relationships, it means that you become what your customer wants you to be. If your customer is thoughtful and deliberate, somber and subdued, be the same things yourself. If your customer is quick and assertive, match his style quip for quip.

When I discuss this concept in my seminars, I often have someone respond with the question, "Isn't that phony?"

The answer is no. Think of yourself as a diamond. You can rotate the diamond to reflect certain facets of yourself that are already there. If you don't have it in you, you can't be something you're not. When you reflect a customer's unique style, you're choosing to reflect and emphasize a certain part of yourself.

You're subjugating your own passing emotions for a decision of will to be disciplined in reflecting your customer's behavior style back to him or her.

Secondly, you are only going to reflect their style, not their beliefs, goals, or values. For example, if one of your customers is a Democrat and you're a Republican, you are not going to pretend that you're a Democrat. That would be phony. You don't change who you are. Rather, you choose to accommodate someone else's style. It's not an issue of content, it's an issue of form.

When you think about this concept a bit, you'll probably discover that you're already doing this in other aspects of your life. You talk to your children differently than you speak to your parents. Why is that? Because you understand that different communication styles work with different people. That same principle is true in business relationships, also.

This skill of reflective behavior merely asks you to systematize and improve some things that you're probably doing to some extent already. Your challenge is to do it more consistently and effectively.

People buy from people they like. People like people who are like themselves. So, be like them. If you're like them, they'll feel comfortable with you, and be more likely to enter into a preferred relationship.

Once you begin to think this way, it's easy to do. The key is to accurately reflect your customer's style back to him or her.

Think of their style as being composed of three different elements: Non-verbal behavior, verbal expressions, and oral cadences. You'll find it helpful to concentrate on reflecting each of these.

Non-verbal behavior describes a person's body language, movements, and posture. Focus on these and reflect them. So, for example, if your customer is leaning forward making quick and excited gestures, when it's your turn to speak, do the same thing. If your customer is leaning back in the chair in a relaxed and confident pose, you do the same thing.

Be subtle about this. You don't want your customer to think that you're mocking him. Rather, you're helping him to be comfortable with you by reflecting the style that he's most comfortable with. Wait a few seconds after your customer switches position, and then slowly reflect that body language.

This is sometimes difficult for us to do, because our natural instinct is to do exactly the opposite. If, for example, your customer is speaking slowly and softly, you may want to move him along more quickly. So, you speak quickly and to the point. By so doing, however, you make the customer feel pressured and inject tension in the dialogue.

One of my seminar participants related an excellent example of this principle in use. She was attending one of my five-session courses, and took the presentation about reflective behavior to heart. At the beginning of the next session, she was excited to share her experience.

"I have been calling unsuccessfully on a prospect," she said, "and I couldn't seem to make any headway with her. One of the problems was that the prospect wouldn't make eye contact with me. So, I would try to get her to look me in the eye. It was very frustrating talking to her. Then, after your presentation about reflective behavior last week, I decided to try it. So, when I called on her this time, I consciously did not make eye contact with her. I reflected her non-verbal behavior. And I walked out with an order for the first time!"

It's a great story and an excellent illustration of the principle of reflecting non-verbal behavior.

You should also reflect the customer's verbal expressions. Every customer has a certain vocabulary and a set of figures of speech with which they are most comfortable. Be sensitive to the language your customer uses, and use those same expressions and words when it's your turn to speak.

I recall meeting for the first time with a CEO of a distribution company who would later become one of my closest clients. He was at first somewhat defensive about his organization. His company was struggling to efficiently handle a large quantity of small orders. He chose to talk about the problem in this way:

"It's like we're in the middle of the river, trying to swim against the current. All these small orders are washing over us, making it almost impossible to make any progress."

I chose to respond to him like this: "It sounds to me like we need to build some water sluices and dams in order to control the flow."

"That's it exactly!" he shouted.

I could have said that he should develop some process controls and internal procedures to deal with the issue, but instead I chose to reflect his language and use his analogies and expressions back to him. When I did so, I sent him the message that I understood, and I was like him. That was the beginning of a long and mutually beneficial relationship.

Finally, be sensitive to your customer's oral cadence, and

reflect that also. The word "cadence" refers to the rhythm and power in the customer's voice. It has little to do with what is said, rather it focuses on the way it was said.

As you concentrate on this aspect of a person's communication style, you'll find that some people speak slowly, thinking about every word. Others are sharp and to the point and accent every other word. There are as many cadences as there are people.

I recall calling on a regional Vice President of a large national distributor. His office was in an old grocery store on the outskirts of a small mid-western city. As the receptionist led me into his office, I noticed an old office partition leaning up against the wall. On it was pinned a sales graph. There were no other decorations in the office, and it was bare except for a perfectly clean steel desk, and two chairs that did not match.

He shook my hand quickly and said, "What can I do for you?"

My response was as terse and to the point as his question. "I have three items on my agenda" I said. "Here they are."

I attempted to reflect back to him the style that he was comfortable with. That meant using the cadence that he used with me.

Over the past 20 years, a great deal of work has been done by psychologists interested in "behavior styles." And, while most of them differ in their choice of terms, they generally agree on the basic formulas for classifying people. My description is a compilation of a number of different authors.

Think of rating people on two different scales. The first has to do with their mode of communication. At one end of the scale are people who are very direct. They don't beat around the bush or put things in soft ways.

I recall a crusty old materials manager who was a great example of this end of the scale. His first comments to me were:

"We have too many vendors right now. We don't need any more. We don't know much about your company, but what we've heard we don't like." He didn't beat around the bush. That's direct and to the point.

On the other end of the scale are indirect people who tell you something like: "Oh yeah, call me next week. Sure." But what they really mean is, "I'm never going to buy this, but I can't bring myself to say no."

Now, imagine a scale that goes from the very direct type of person to the very indirect. This scale measures the way a person is most comfortable in communicating to the outside world. Everyone in the world, including yourself and all of your customers, can be placed somewhere on the scale.

Now, imagine another scale. This one measures the way people are most comfortable receiving information. We call this trait "closed" or "open." Closed people are extremely task oriented. Open people are very people oriented. Just as with the first scale, everyone in the world can be classified somewhere along the line of "openness."

If we overlay these two scales on top of each other at right angles we create a cross with four quadrants. We can characterize people in each of these quadrants on how they fit on the scale of closed/open, and direct/indirect.

Look at Illustration # 6. By plotting the coordinates of the two scales, we place a person in one of the four quadrants.

That placement can tell us a great deal about a person. Over the years, a number of authors and researchers have studied these four different types of people, and added greatly to our understanding of them.

A person who fits into the upper left quadrant, for example, is often called a director or controller. The primary need of this kind of person is to dominate.

Behavioral Styles

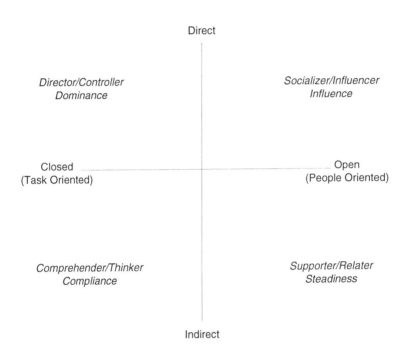

Illustration #6

Some people are very direct yet open — socializers or motivators. Their primary motivation is to influence. Those are the people who fall into the upper right quadrant.

Bottom left quadrant people are closed and indirect, and are characterized by names like comprehender or thinker. Their primary motive is to comply.

In the bottom right quadrant are people who are often called supporters or relators. Their primary motivation is steadiness.

Thinkers like to build relationships. They are friendly and likable, and often have traditional attitudes. They make very careful decisions and appear wishy-washy.

The very first sales job I had in my life was selling men's suits in a very good men's clothing store as a way of working my way through college. I was fortunate enough to work for a great boss who was an excellent sales manager. He told me to watch out for pipe smokers (this was in the '60s). He said, "Don't wait on a pipe smoker. They never make up their mind. They will keep considering the purchase, talk about it, waste hours of your time and then walk out and not make a decision." My experience later proved him right.

The pipe smoker was the archetypal "thinker." These people make very careful decisions and appear wishy-washy. To work effectively with this kind of person, be friendly, and build support for your proposition quickly. Don't pressure them. Stress the emotional benefits because they'll forever weigh the intellectual merits of the decision. Allow them to include others in their decisions. That's their style.

Supporters are on the other end of the quadrant. They like numbers and figures, facts and detail, and are money and time oriented. They are also risk averse.

The stereotypical purchasing agent is a good example of this personality type. Deal with them effectively by letting them feel they are right. Give them facts. Stress the rational and logical reasons. Complement them regularly. Use a quick and direct close. Both of these types like details and specifics and are generally slow in moving.

On the other hand, consider controllers. They tell you things. They don't ask you. They speak loudly. They move quickly and make direct eye contact. Sometimes you almost feel like they are staring you down. They lean toward you, gesture a lot and finish your sentences for you. They are serious and formal.

To work effectively with controllers, get right to the point — don't waste time. Put everything in writing; they don't trust you. Summarize the key benefits, use an alternative close. This puts the power in their hands. They want control.

Influencers will ask personal questions. They are friendly, and may touch you. A director or controller would not get close enough, physically. That's a good clue. They make many hand movements but not with the same kind of power that a controller does.

Present the big picture to the influencers. Use emotional benefits, recognize them as being important, use a reassuring and direct close.

Making People Comfortable With You

You've heard the saying that you never get a second chance to make a first impression. That is absolutely true, and incredibly important to salespeople. Often, your customer or prospect will subconsciously decide in the first few minutes of your conversation whether or not he likes you. Or, whether or not he is going to interact with you honestly, spend more time with you, and trust you.

These aren't necessarily conscious decisions, although they can be. Usually, it's more like a quick judgement that takes place within the first few minutes. So, the first few minutes of an interaction are incredibly important.

Here are three things to do to use those first few minutes effectively.

1. Show interest in them. One of the most powerful things you can do when meeting someone for the first time is to show interest in that person. It makes him feel appreciated and he, in turn, responds by being interested in you. It's the law of reciprocity — one of the most powerful laws governing human behavior. It says that people will act towards you the way you first act towards them.

You know that from your own experience. What happens when you've had a miserable day, and you come home and slam the door, kick the dog, and throw your briefcase into the room? Does your spouse lovingly say, "Oh, I'm so glad you're home?" Probably not. He or she will act towards you the way *you* first acted.

The law of reciprocity also governs sales relationships. If you demonstrate interest in your prospect, he will be drawn to you.

Take a couple of seconds, when you first walk into someone's office or place of business, and find something to be interested in. People arrange their work environment to express themselves. Your job is to be sensitive to the part of themselves they are expressing by noticing something to be interested in. It could be any one of a number of different things. Pictures of families or outings, magazines and books, certificates and awards, knickknacks, all of these indicate something your prospect is interested in, and therefore something that you can ask about. Ask sincere questions about one of those things, and you'll get the prospect talking about himself, and feeling positive about you.

Sometimes it's impossible to notice something in the environment because you meet someone in a place other than his/her own personal work area. In that case, you must pay close attention to the person and the way he presents himself.

I recall a great example of this. I was meeting someone for the first time in a lobby area. As I shook hands with him, I noticed that he had a large pinky ring that was constructed of turquoise and silver. Then I noticed a watchband on his other hand that was similarly constructed. Now, obviously, there was a story behind those adornments.

2. Find common ground. The sooner you can find something you have in common with your prospect, the quicker will you begin to develop a relationship with him and make him comfortable with you.

So, as you look around to find something to be interested in, see if you can also find something that you have in common with the prospect. You may have been to the same place, traveled or gone on vacations to the same area, gone to the same church, rooted for the same sports teams, belonged to the same civic organizations, seen the same movies, read the same books, seen the same plays, or known the same people. Got the idea? The sooner you find something you have in common, the sooner you'll put the prospect at ease and make him comfortable with you.

Here's an example of how this works in real life. I went into a man's office, a CEO of a small business, to meet him for the first time. I was there to discuss doing sales training. He asked if I wanted a cup of coffee. By the way, I always take a cup of coffee, even if I've just come from a breakfast meeting, and I've had six cups of coffee already and I am beginning to sweat and wonder where the restroom is.

There's a reason for that. Think about what happens when you say, "Yes, I'll have a cup of coffee." Your host has to arrange for it. He has to either get the coffee, or instruct someone else to get it. In either case, he has to take a few moments to attend to the task. While he's doing that, you can use that time to look around the office and find something to be interested in.

That's exactly what happened. When he was out making arrangements for coffee, I spotted a large photograph of a sailboat. I sail. So, I immediately chose that as the item in which I would be interested, and my point of common ground.

When he came in and handed me the coffee, the first think I did was point at the photograph and say "You sail?" He replied, "Yes, that's my boat." The photograph was large enough that I could make out the name of the boat. It was "Kelly Ann." I have a daughter named Kelly Ann. Which is what I said to him next. And he said, "I have daughter named Kelly Ann. This boat was named after her."

At that point, the conversation turned to daughters and sailing, and we achieved a real, common bond based on our similar interests and experiences. None of this would have happened had I not disciplined myself to find common ground and be interested in him.

3. Share something personal and unique about yourself. When you meet a prospect for the first time, particularly in the first few minutes, he tends to treat you as a stereotype. You're a "salesperson," not a real person. As long as you allow yourself to be treated as a stereotype, you'll maintain a superficial, stereotypical relationship. Change that by breaking though the wall between your prospect and yourself. You can accomplish this by sharing something unique and personal about yourself.

Here's an example. During the first few minutes of most meetings I have with a new prospect, I try to work into the conversation the fact that my wife and I are foster parents. We have, over the years, cared for 18 foster children.

You're probably asking what that has to do with sales. My answer is, "Nothing." But if you ask what it has to do with creating a relationship with the prospect, getting him to see me as a real, live human being, then I'd say it has *everything* to do with that.

You see, once I share something unique and personal about myself, that I'm a foster father, the prospect can no longer treat me as a stereotype. He now sees me as a *real* person with *real* blood flowing through my veins.

You can do the same thing.

Use any or all of these introductory techniques to get the relationship off to a good start, and get a head start on your competition.

To implement the ideas
in this chapter...

1. List each of the key decision makers in each of your "A" accounts. Think about their behavioral styles, and label each one as a director, influencer, thinker, or supporter.

2. Decide how you should vary your behavior to reflect each of their comfortable behavioral styles.

3. Resolve to find something to be interested in with every new person you meet.

4. Resolve to strive to find common ground with every new account.

5. Resolve to share something personal about yourself with every new person you meet.

Chapter Eight
Transferable Sales Skills – Part One: What Are You Really Selling?

My first professional sales position was with a company that manufactured and sold a line of amplification equipment for classrooms of hearing-impaired children. The sales training consisted of four weeks of intense work in California. I spent every day learning about the product and practicing my presentations word-for-word. By the time I was finished with the training program, I could give the sales presentation forward and backward. I knew how to sell the product, and I knew each product intimately.

Unfortunately, I really didn't know much about salesmanship. I just knew how to sell that particular product.

That experience was repeated years later when I accepted a position selling surgical staplers. Again, it involved working for a manufacturer that sold directly to the end user. And, again, I went off to the coast, this time to Manhattan, where I practiced using the instruments and memorizing the pitch. When I left, I was sufficiently prepared to go into surgery and verbally assist a surgeon in the use and application of the instruments. I was extremely well prepared to sell those instruments, but woefully under-instructed in general sales concepts and techniques.

Selling for most companies follows that same path. You can learn the intricacies of the sales presentation for a particular product or service, and you can be successful by utilizing those techniques and words — without ever having a grasp of general sales principles.

But *you* don't have that luxury. You're presented with thousands of different items you're expected to sell. And you're expected to do so without the benefit of weeks of intensive training.

That means that you must have a better understanding of sales principles and concepts than your manufacturer rep friends. And, you must have a set of skills that you can transfer from one product to another. You need to be equipped with a powerful set of *transferable sales skills.*

What does a distributor sell?

Let's start by considering what a distributor really sells. Think of an onion. Slice that onion in half so that you have a cross section that looks like Illustration # 7. If you were peeling that onion, and you started at the outermost layer, you'd notice that it was thin and dry, and not very pungent. However, as you peeled away each succeeding layer of the onion, you'd soon learn that the strength of the onion's pungency comes from the inside out.

So it is with the kinds of things a distributor sells. Sometimes, you just sell *price.* In other words, you tell purchasing agents or buyers that you can provide the exact same product for a little less money than they are currently paying. Or, you respond to a bid with the lowest price and capture the busi-

What Does a Distributor Sell?

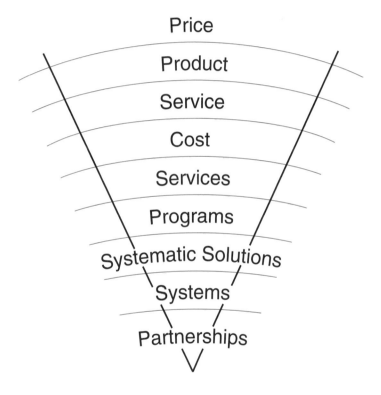

Illustration #7

ness. In that case, you've also sold *price*. It's the easiest thing to sell, and the most superficial. If you only sell *price*, you remain on the most superficial layer of your relationship with your customer, much like the outer skin of an onion. If you want to be successful, you must sell things that are closer to the heart of the account.

Go a little bit deeper, and you'll be selling *product*. When you do that, you spend your time demonstrating and detailing products. You continuously select new products to show your customers, and you keep a variety of products in front of them.

That's much of what distributor salespeople do. It's much of what I did when I built my territory from $100,000 to over $5 million in less than five years. And, while you need to do some of that, there are other things you must sell if you're going to excel in the new economy.

If you focus on only selling *price* and *product*, you remain on a superficial level with your customers. That strategy, particularly the price strategy, makes you vulnerable to competition. There will always be someone who can sell it for less. Not only that, but your hot new product will soon be outdated. So, focusing exclusively on price and product leaves you in a most vulnerable position.

But there's another problem that is just as critical. Selling product is *very* labor intensive. You must usually make several sales calls and become involved in demonstrating and presenting the product. Then you have to train end users. In addition, you must invest your time to learn about the product before you can sell it. That's a lot of time invested in something that may soon be obsolete.

So let's penetrate deeper into the onion. Take the issue one layer deeper, and you'll find *service*. Now we're getting into the regions that distributors are best equipped to travel with a customer. By *service* I mean the kinds of measurements that distributors like to brag about. Fill rates, percentage of backorders, credits issued, etc. When you're at this level with a customer, you're talking with him about your company's superior performance in filling orders promptly and accurately. That's a deeper issue than just product or price.

The next level is *cost.* Cost is broader and deeper than the others. Cost refers to a conversation you have with the customer about his total cost of acquiring, storing, dispensing and using the combination of products you sell. The price he pays is only one component of cost. The types of products you sell, the service levels you provide, all combine to impact the customer's total costs.

For example, suppose your competitor sells a product by the pallet load only, and you provide it by the case. The customer gets it 5 percent cheaper from your competitor. But, he has to buy more of it, store it, insure it while it's in his warehouse, and handle it more frequently. This all adds to his cost. In this case, even though the competitor's *price* is less, your effect on lowering the customer's total *cost* may be greater.

The next level of depth refers to selling services. Services refers to the things you do for the customer that he could do himself. For example, let's say you sell a combination of six products designed to be used in various combinations. With the sale, you agree to take a monthly inventory, and provide the customer with a list of the items and quantities he should reorder.

Inventory and requisition is a service you provide that the customer could and probably did do himself. These services range from some simple things like taking inventory, to very sophisticated computer interfaces and logistics management, to seminars and training programs.

Next is *programs.* Programs are combinations of products and services. They represent ways to sell more than just one product to the customer. For example, when you show your customer how a series of products from one or more manufacturers complement one another, and then offer them together with a special service your company has created, you're offering a program.

The next level is *systematic solutions.* In a sense, every product or service you sell is a solution to some need or problem. However, at this level, I'm talking about major solutions to systematic problems. This level of problem requires you to understand the customer's business in ways that are almost impossible for a manufacturer because it requires strong relationships with a variety of people throughout the customer organization.

It also requires you to creatively package your services and products in a way that helps the customer with systematic processes.

The next level is *systems.* A system is a negotiated agreement — a contract — where you and your customer negotiate almost every detail of the relationship between you. Total dollar volume of sales, gross profits, your service levels, payment terms, how many orders will be placed electronically, delivery terms, and so forth. A systems contract can take a long time to negotiate, and it requires an intense and broad relationship with the customer.

The final level of depth is *partnership.* A partnership exists when you and your customer grow to depend on and trust one another so thoroughly that your success is intertwined. As your customer grows, so do you. As you grow, your customer benefits. Your customer comes to rely on you as an integral, hard to replace part of his business.

Our turbulent times will find more and more competitors struggling to compete at the outer layers. If, however, you're going to excel at distributor sales, you'll need to push the conversations in your accounts to the deepest levels. While you may always have to sell at all levels, the deeper levels represent your best opportunities for profit, security and challenge. You'll need to have some partnerships to provide for your long-term security. It'll be difficult to have more than 5 percent of your total customer base in this category, but the more partners you're able to develop, the more effective you'll be.

You'll need even more systems relationships, because they are on their way to becoming partners with you. As you move up towards the outer layers, you'll find yourself selling relatively more of each level.

In one sense, there is a longevity element to this. When you first begin a relationship with a customer, you often start with price or product. As you penetrate the account more deeply, and grow in your relationship with each account, you can sell the deeper items. It may take years to reach partnership status with some accounts.

There is also a relationship component to getting to the deeper levels. You really can't sell effectively at the deeper levels unless you have great relationships. And, they don't come quickly or with everyone.

As a distributor salesperson, you need to be able to sell at all of these levels. You'll probably always have to sell product and price to some degree. However, if you're going to be effective in our turbulent times, you'll need to move each customer deeper in their relationship with you. That means that you must continue to try to sell each customer at ever deeper levels.

And that requires you to be well equipped with transferable sales skills.

As we begin to examine the crucial transferable sales skills, let's begin at the first part of your sales task — getting to see the people you need to see.

Planning for Effective Appointment Setting

Some of the bad news for salespeople working in our turbulent times is that it is more difficult than ever to make appointments with the people you need to see. Your customers have less time today than they did a few years ago. They aren't as available as they used to be. That means that they're not as open to you just stopping by. And that means that you must make formal appointments much more frequently than before.

But that's not all the bad news. Voice mail has made it very difficult to get through to the people with whom you want to speak.

Those ripples in the currents mean that you have to consider the task of making appointments as a special discipline. Here's how to do it more effectively.

First, take a few minutes to think about your prospect. What is he doing when you call? What is he concerned about? What is occupying his mind? Why would he be motivated to talk to you? With a clear picture of your prospect in your mind, you're better equipped to approach that person.

Next, if you're dealing with a prospect who doesn't know you, or only knows you slightly, you may want to consider creating a "pre-call touch." That's a communication to your prospect either from or about you.

For example, if you write a letter to your prospect, that's a pre-call touch. If you have one of your customers write to him, that is also a pre-call touch.

Pre-call touches can take a number of forms. You can write a letter, fax a message, E-mail, send a series of letters, mail a newsletter, deliver a package, deliver a series of packages, or have someone else do all those things for you.

The key thing in your pre-call touch is that you give the

prospect some reason to take your call. Remember, you're not selling your product, you're selling the appointment. Say something in the letter that will make your prospect want to talk with you.

Once you've delivered your pre-call touch, you're ready to call the prospect.

However, before you call, it's wise to prepare for every possible eventually. You may have only one chance at a conversation with this person. If you blow it, you may not have another opportunity for years.

That means that you had better prepare what you're going to say. Prepare an outline, or even a word-for-word script.

Think about what may happen when you phone the prospect. There are three situations to be prepared for.

One possibility is that you'll get a "gatekeeper." That's someone who can open the door to let you in to see the person you want to talk to, or close the door to keep you out. They're the keepers of the gate to the person you want to speak with. Usually, receptionists, secretaries, and assistants fulfill this role. Another possibility is that you'll reach voice mail, and be told to leave a recorded message. Finally, there is the possibility that you'll reach the right person — the one you want to talk to.

Let's talk about how to prepare for each eventuality. If you reach a gatekeeper, your best strategy is to make them allies. In other words, don't try to intimidate them, don't dismiss them, don't try to power through them. Instead, make them allies. Learn their names, and use them. Explain why the boss should talk to you, and what benefit it would be to him. Then ask politely if they'll put you through to the boss.

If you reach voice mail, you also need to be prepared. There are several strategies that you may want to pursue. First, always leave a message. Every time your prospect hears your name, or a message from you, it's one more repetitive exposure, just like an advertising message. So, make sure you always leave a message.

Organize your message like a memo. Briefly state who it's to, who it's from, the content, and the benefit of returning the call. Remember, you're not selling your product at this point. You're not even selling an appointment. You're just selling a phone call. So give your prospect a reason for returning your call.

Another option is to phrase your call like a personalized 30 second radio advertisement. If you could beam a personal radio advertisement to your prospect just for him, and focus that advertisement on prompting him to call you, what would be in that ad? That's exactly what voice mail allows you to do. Look at it as an opportunity to beam a radio message to your prospect. Send one every day until he calls back.

Here's a novel approach. Make the appointment. That's right. Leave a message on voice mail saying that you'll see him at such and such a time, unless you hear from him otherwise. Then do it. You'll be surprised at how many people will either call back to change the appointment, or keep it.

Hopefully, your hard work will result in your finally getting on the phone with the right person. You have worked too hard up to this point to blow it now.

Be prepared for the moment when you have someone on the phone. You'll need to have a script or, at the very least, an outline of the things you want to say. The script or outline should contain these components:

- **Introduction.** Who you are (first and last name), where you're calling from (location — particularly if you're calling long distance), and the name of your company. If your company may be unknown to him, a short description of what your company does is appropriate.

- **Purpose.** Why you are calling. Specifically, what you want to see him about.

- **Benefit.** Why he should see you. What's in it for him?

- **Qualify.** Ask a question that gets the person into the conversation and qualifies him as a worthwhile prospect. In some cases, you may want to move this question up to the beginning of the script.

- **Time Commitment.** How much time will you need to convey your benefit?

- **Close.** Ask for the appointment.

At this point, you're engaged in a classic closing situation, and all the strategies and tactics discussed in Chapter Eleven (Closing) apply here.

The single best thing to do is to prepare for objections you may hear. Study the section on handling objections (Chapter Eleven) and apply those principles at this time. Ask yourself, "What are the most likely objections I'll hear? How should I respond to them?"

When you've done these things, you're ready to make appointments effectively.

To implement the ideas in this chapter...

1. Compare the presentations you have made in the last 30 days with the levels of depth in Illustration #7. Have you made presentations at the deeper levels?

2. Look at every proposal you make in the near future, and consider how to rewrite it to present one level deeper.

3. Create an effective pre-call touch for your next cold call.

4. Create an appointment-making script for voice mail, for a gatekeeper, and for the right person.

Chapter Nine

Transferable Sales Skills — Part Two: Managing an Interactive Sales Dialogue

The heart of the sales process is your conversation with your customers and prospects. It's that moment in time, when you are face to face with the customer, that defines the uniqueness of your position, and distinguishes you from all the others who work for your company.

Think about it. You're practically the only one in your company who meets face to face with the customer. If it weren't for that, you'd be unnecessary.

So, it behooves you to think about how to do it well. First, let's think about the most basic steps of the sales process. Boil them down to their simplest components. What you do with your prospect or customer is this:

- You make them comfortable with you.

- You find out what they want.

- You show how what you have helps them get what they want.

- You get their agreement to acquire it.

That simple four-step process can takes months to complete, or it can be whisked through in two minutes. But its basically what you do as a salesperson. It's the process that your boss pays you to master.

Let's think about the process and consider how to master it. It stands to reason that, if you can master that quintessential task that defines your job, then you can master sales.

Several years ago, I would have described this interchange as *making a sales presentation*. But that term emphasizes one-way communication — you talking to the customer — and that's just not effective.

So, now I describe this process as *managing a sales interaction*. *Managing* describes your major role. Your primary role is not a presenter of information. Rather, your primary role is to manage the communication process between you and your customer. What happens between you and your customer is solely and entirely *your* responsibility. Like a manager is responsible for the processes in his department, so you are responsible for the communication process between you and your customer.

Interactive refers to the notion that the communication is two-way, not one-way. It consists of conversation between you and your customer. Without conversation from your customer, the sales process is not viable. Selling isn't telling. If anything, the more your customer talks, and the less talking you do, the more effective the sales call is.

Sales refers to the fact that this communication is moving toward an agreement between the two of you. When you're passing the time of day with your spouse, or engaging in light banter at a cocktail party, it's not a sales dialogue. It's purpose is not to come to agreement. The definition of sales is: influencing a prospect to come to an *agreement* with you to purchase something you offer. The agreement is the main thing. So, this conversation is a sales conversation because it focuses on coming to an agreement.

Finally, it's a *dialogue*. That means it's an honest exchange of feeling, facts, values, and perceptions. The depth and quality of that interaction and communication is the distinguishing standard.

How do you manage an interactive sales dialogue so that the chances of its success are enhanced?

Let's start by comparing the process to a baseball game. Illustration # 8 graphically describes the process. You know how baseball is played. If you're the batter, you start by taking your position in the on-deck circle. There you wait for your opportunity to get to bat. If you never get to the batter's box, you never have an opportunity to score.

If you're fortunate, you get to the batter's box. Now you have an opportunity to make a hit and score a run. If you're good, and you make a hit, you run to first base. If you successfully negotiate first base, you then move to second base. From second you move to third. At his point, how many runs have you scored? Obviously, none. Nothing counts until you make it home.

Now, let's compare this process to our interactive sales dialogue. You first need to move from the on-deck circle to the batter's box. That occurs when you establish some rapport with the customer and make him feel comfortable with you. Without that, you have very little opportunity to go further.

Once you get to the batter's box, you next have to hit the ball. That means that you are able to focus the communication process on the subject at hand — your customer's needs and your ability to meet them.

The next step is to get to first base. First base in the sales process is understanding the customer's needs and interests. I call that combination of needs and interests — what the cus-

Managing an Interactive Sales Dialogue

Interactive: Questions and answers.
Sales: Purpose is to come to agreement on some course of action.
Dialogue: Honest exchange of ideas, perceptions, feelings and facts.

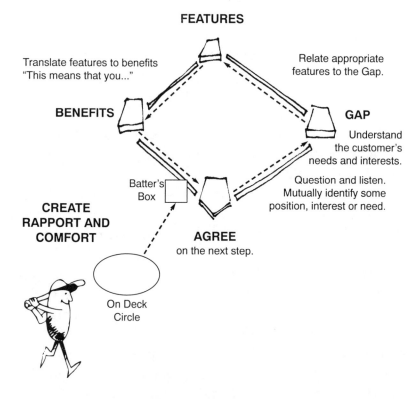

Illustration #8

tomer wants — the *Gap*. The Gap describes what is missing in the customer's business that you can provide.

Just like you can't go to second base until you've made it to first safely, so you can't really talk about your product or services until you successfully understand your customer's needs. You accomplish this primarily by asking good questions, and listening constructively.

Now, you're ready to move to second base. You arrive at second base when you finally earn the opportunity to point out the features of your product or service. From that point you move quickly to third base, which requires you to translate those features into benefits.

Finally, to score a run, you have to safely negotiate home plate. In the sales process, that means that you successfully acquire an agreement from your customer for the next step or the action that both of you will take as a result of your dialogue.

To a great degree, your success as a distributor salesperson will be dependent on your ability to successfully manage interactive sales dialogues over and over again with your customers and prospects.

Let's think about how to do it well. Getting to the batter's box means that you have created a feeling of comfort and trust in the customer. That's a necessary prerequisite for going further. You don't get a chance to even take a swing unless you've done that.

The techniques we discussed in Chapter Seven for building relationships are those that you can employ in the early part of a sales dialogue to create comfort and interest.

Then, you must concentrate on understanding what the customer wants or needs. That involves understanding his Gap.

Understanding the Gap

What's a Gap?

It's the combination of needs and interests in the customer that drives him to consider your company or product in the first place. I like to characterize it as *what's missing*. In other words, something is missing in the company or person you're calling on, or they wouldn't want to talk to you. For example, if I go buy a can of Pepsi, what was the Gap that drove me to that action? If you're thinking "thirst," you're right. Understanding what's missing in your customer, or the Gap, is the essential step to being able to adequately present your company, and it's programs, solutions and products.

The Gap can be either positive or negative. When it's positive, we call it a drive for something worthwhile that the person wants but doesn't have. For example, your customer may want to increase his sales or profits. There's nothing wrong with his current level of sales, he just wants to increase them. That's a goal, or a positive Gap.

When the Gap is negative, it's a matter of solving some problem the customer has, or alleviating some pain. For example, let's say your customer has a piece of production equipment that keeps breaking down, causing down-time on a production line. That's a problem. He wants to solve that problem and alleviate the pain caused by the troublesome machine.

Understanding the customer's Gap thoroughly and deeply is one of the key sales skills that separate the mediocre salespeople from the masters. In fact, the ability to more thoroughly and completely understand the customer's Gap is one of the distinguishing advantages the distributor salesperson has over the manufacturer and all the other non-traditional channels. No other competing vendor has the ability to understand the customer as well as you do, because no other competing salesperson calls on that individual as frequently as you do.

What Do You Know About Your Customers?

Illustration #9

Look at Illustration # 9. It's that onion illustration again, only this time it refers to layers of depth in understanding your customer. On the very surface are the technical specifications for the product or service the customer wants. For example, let's say you call on one of your customers and he says, "I need to purchase three green metal widgets that are 1/2" by 6". Many distributor salespeople would say, "OK, I've got X brand for $2.50 and Y brand for $3.15, which would you rather have?" In this example, the distributor rep understood the Gap at the most superficial level — technical specifications— and responded in kind.

But you can go deeper in understanding the customers's Gap by discovering the reason behind those specifications.

Our rep, when confronted with the same request, may say, "What are you going to use them for?" or, "Is there a reason you asked for metal instead of plastic?" This kind of response will uncover the next level of Gap, the *reason* for the specifications.

There's more. *Situation* refers to the history behind the need, and the circumstances surrounding the need. For example, let's say that our distributor rep now replies, "John, what's your situation? Why is this an issue now?" When the customer replies to that question, he has uncovered a deeper layer of need.

Yet you're still pretty close to the surface. When you uncover the specific problems and objectives which underlay the original request, you've gotten deeper in your understanding of the Gap. Back to our example. Suppose your customer says, "We're having a problem with our second shift production. The line keeps breaking down. Our maintenance supervisor wants to stockpile some of the parts that he has been regularly replacing."

Now you have an understanding of the specific problems and objectives. There is more. Suppose you ask how that problem affects the rest of the company. And suppose your customer explains the effect of the breakdown on production, net profits, and overtime pay for the second shift. Now you understand the customer's Gap at yet a deeper level.

But you can go deeper still. When you ask how those systematic problems affect his business goals, and you learn that it's particularly troublesome because your customer's goals are to increase net profits by 5 percent this year, you understand the customer's Gap at an even deeper level.

You take a significant plunge deeper when you are able to understand how the Gap affects the individual with whom you're talking. For example, when you know him well enough to ask, "John, how can I make you look good in this transaction?" and get an honest response, you've penetrated to a new layer of understanding.

Finally, when you understand the individual motivations — the reasons for the personal factors — you understand the customer's Gap at levels that few salespeople ever approach. That's where the masters work.

As you think about this concept, you'll probably make several inferences. First, it takes time and work to move to the deeper levels of understanding. You can't expect to penetrate to the deepest levels in just one conversation. It's just not the way people work. In fact, in a large account, it may take you a year or more, and literally hundreds of conversations with various people, to come to a precise and deep understanding of the Gap.

You generally don't have the time to dig that deeply with everyone. The first rule is, therefore, to spend your "Gap-digging" time only with those accounts that have the highest potential.

But there's a second rule. While you can't invest large amounts of time in every account, you can concentrate on digging deeper with every call you make. For example, you may have decided to spend your quality time with four or five accounts. This is where you try to meet all the department heads, the vice presidents, the controller, the material manager, and so forth. Keep copious notes (see Account Profiles), and do a lot of strategizing for these accounts.

But you still have 50 other accounts that don't get that kind of attention. What can you do with them? Rule Three: Dig deeper each time. You can't take the time to try to meet the controller and the other department heads but, when you are talking to your primary contact, you can dig as deeply as possible.

Remember the discussion in the last chapter about what a distributor actually sells? Price and product are the most superficial offerings, and systems and partnerships are the deepest. There is a direct relationship between your ability to know your customer at deeper levels and your ability to sell the deeper, more intense "products." Look at illustration # 10.

Notice the relationship between the level at which you know your customer, and your ability to provide deeper levels of product and service.

While the relationship isn't exactly one to one as the illustration would imply, it is generally true that your ability to sell deeper services to your customer depends directly on your ability to know him better.

What You Know About The Customer

What You Can Sell

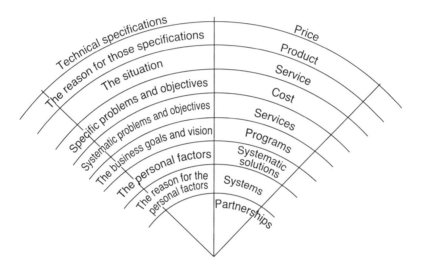

Illustration #10

To implement the ideas in this chapter...

1. Structure your next presentation around the baseball diamond format.

2. Pick one of the presentations that you made recently. Think about which level of the customer's Gap you were aware of before you made the presentation.

3. List all of your "A" accounts. Think about each, and try to describe their Gap at each level of depth described in Illustration 8.

4. Describe a couple ways you can dig deeper prior to making your next presentation.

Chapter Ten
Transferable Sales Skills —
Part Three: The Art of
Asking Questions

Did you enjoy what you had for dinner last night? I know, you're wondering what that has to do with sales. Bear with me a moment, and answer the question.

Now, step back a second, and think about what you did when you read that question. Your mind probably flashed back to yesterday evening, and you saw a picture in your mind's eye of what you had for dinner. And then you recalled your response to the dinner, and made a judgment that you did or didn't enjoy it.

Here's the point to this exercise. I was able to *direct your thinking* by asking you a question. That's an illustration of the power of a question. A well-phrased, appropriately-timed question directs a person's thinking. Similarly, the right question penetrates your prospect's mind and directs his thinking. It's the single most powerful tool any salesperson has.

It's almost impossible to be asked a question and not think of the answer. I'm not sure whether it's something in our basic humanity, or if we're conditioned since birth to always think of the answer to a question. Here's an illustration. I'll ask you a question, but I want you to *not* think of the answer. How old are you? If you're like most of us, you thought of the answer, even after I indicated you shouldn't. There is something in all of us that makes us think of the answer when we're asked a question. To not do so takes a steel will and great discipline.

Now, consider where the decision to buy your products or services takes place. It happens in the mind of your prospect. That's one reason why a question is such a powerful tool. It directs and shapes the direction in which your prospect's mind works.

Here's an illustration. Let's say you go to buy a new car. The salesperson asks you, "Which is more important to you, good fuel economy, or quick pickup?" Until asked, you haven't really thought of it that way. The salesperson's question helps you understand what you really think, and directs your mind along a certain course.

A good question is your best means of collecting the information that will help you construct a sale. How do you know what a prospect thinks, or what his situation is, unless you ask a question? It helps you to see what's in the mind of your prospect. Questions provide you with information.

A question is also a powerful tool to show that you care about the person and his problems. The more questions you ask, the more your prospect feels you're interested in him. The law of reciprocity indicates that the more interest you show in a prospect, the more likely it is that he'll be interested in you.

Finally, a series of good questions reinforces the perception of your competence. In other words, your prospect sees you as competent and trustworthy — not necessarily by what you say — but rather by what you ask.

Here's an illustration. Let's say you have a problem with your car. You take it into the mechanic down the street and say to him, "My car is making a funny sound." He says to you, "OK, leave it here and pick it up at five."

You're not reassured by his approach, so you take it to the mechanic across the street. You say the same thing to him. And he says to you, "What kind of sound?" You reply, "A strange thumping sound." And he says "Is it coming from the front or the back of the car?" And you say, "It's coming from the front." And he asks, "Is it a metallic kind of sound or a rubber kind of sound?" You reply, "It's definitely metallic." And he says, "Does it go faster when you go faster and slower when you go slower, or is it the same speed all the time?" You respond, "It definitely speeds up as I do."

Then he says, "OK, leave it here and pick it up at five." Now, which mechanic seems to be the more competent one? That's an easy question. Obviously, the one who asked more questions. Got the idea? The focus and precision of your questions does more to give your prospect the perception of your competence than anything else.

Questions can be used at every phase of the sales process, but are particularly effective:

- In the initial probing meeting to "open" the sale and understand the customer.

- During your presentation to gather feedback from the customer.

- Following the presentation to achieve agreement on a course of action.

There are five steps to using questions effectively. Illustration # 11 describes them. Let's consider each step.

Five Steps To
Using Questions Successfully

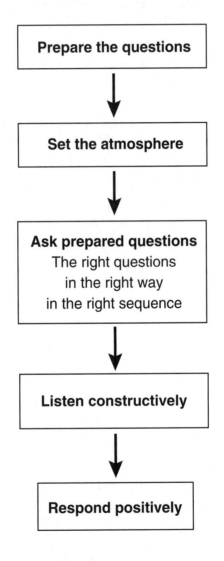

Illustration #11

Prepare the Questions

Spend time preparing the questions you're going to use prior to actually speaking with your customer. You'll be much more likely to phrase them in the best way than if you attempt to do all your composing on the spur of the moment. That's not to say that you'll never create impromptu questions during the interview. Of course you will. But you need to have your basic questions prepared before your meeting starts.

By taking the time to prepare questions first, you plant them into your subconscious mind. And you're much more likely to actually ask the questions you want if you have rehearsed them mentally.

Here's how to prepare them.

First, imagine the situation that you're going into. Take a few moments and construct it in your mind. Next, think about what you want to accomplish in that situation. For example, you may be going into the first meeting with a new prospect. What is it that you want to accomplish in this meeting?

Most salespeople would identify these objectives:

- To uncover the prospect's needs and interests

- To qualify them as a potential buyer

- To attempt to set an appointment for a later date

Now that you have these two things in mind, your situation and your objectives, it's time to begin to develop questions that will take you where you want to go.

Brainstorm all the possibilities. Write down one after another — all the questions that you think you might ask.

When you've exhausted the list, go back over it and rewrite those that make the most sense to you. Then, imagine yourself in the situation and try out each of the questions. Rewrite them, and put them in the sequence you think will work. Now you're ready to ask the questions.

After you go through this planning process a few times, you'll find that you're using some questions over and over. Those good, comfortable, questions can be in your tool-box as "stock" questions that you can use repetitively.

Some questions that I've found to be particularly effective include: "Tell me about your business." "What's your situation?" "What would have to change for us to do more business with you?"

As you create your questions, keep the two basic types in mind — open-ended and close-ended. An open-ended question is one which can't be answered by one word. It calls for an explanation, and there is no right or wrong answer. A close-ended question is just the opposite — it calls for a specific bit of information. So, for example, "How do you feel about our proposal?" is an open-ended question, while "Who got the order?" is a close-ended question.

Once you have your questions prepared, it's time for the next step.

Set the Atmosphere

Atmosphere refers to the emotional climate surrounding the interaction between you and your customer. Is he comfortable with you? Are you honest and frank with one another? Is there an atmosphere of trust and respect? That's the kind of atmosphere you'll want to create. Those words describe the kind of emotional atmosphere that is most conducive to having your questions answered thoroughly and honestly.

How do you create that kind of atmosphere? First, concentrate on being what you want your customer to be. If you want him to be honest and thorough with you, you must first be honest and thorough with him. If you want him to be comfortable and trusting with you, you must first be comfortable and trusting with him. Remember the law of reciprocity? It states that people will react to you in a way similar to how you first act toward them. It's at work here, too. The best thing you can do to create a favorable emotional atmosphere is to be those things yourself.

Once you've influenced the emotional atmosphere surrounding the interaction, you're ready to ask your questions.

Ask the Questions Well

Well means in the right sequence, and in the right way. Let's look at sequences first.

Imagine a funnel with a large opening at the top and a small one at the bottom. That's an illustration for one type of questioning sequence. It graphically describes the amount of information, or the open-endedness of the question. You start with an open-ended question or two, and then slowly narrow the focus of the question down more and more precisely until you're asking very focused questions to collect specific information.

A good application of this technique is in a probing meeting where you are identifying the customer's needs and interests. One specific sequence is the "1-2-3" sequence.

Start with one open-ended question. Then pick two topics out of the customer's response to probe more specifically, and ask three questions about each of the responses. Using this sequence of questions will almost always present you with an opportunity to present a solution.

Here's an example.

Let's say you're selling production equipment. You begin the funnel questioning sequence with one open-ended question. "John, tell me about the current state of your production line." John tells you about how they've recently expanded to a second shift, that the line has been breaking down more frequently because of the increased wear and tear on the equipment. You decide to probe two areas — wear and tear on the equipment, and the implication that business is growing because they've gone to two shifts.

You decide to ask three, ever more precise questions about each of those two areas. You say, "It sounds like your business is growing nicely." You pause to turn the statement into a question. John replies, "Yes, we've recently added a major new contract with one of our customers who is doing very well, and three new customers from our representative in the next state."

You phrase your next question. "If things are going that well, are you thinking about investing in upgrading your equipment?" John replies, "Yes, there's talk about it, but we haven't decided what to do yet." You next phrase the third question of this sequence. "It might help your decision-making process to have some information about the latest equipment. Should I spend some time with you and the engineer to show you what some of your options are?"

John replies, "Probably wouldn't be a bad idea."

You have just used the funnel sequence, specifically, the 1-2-3 version, to identify an opportunity to present a piece of equipment. It's been my experience that the 1-2-3 sequence, in the hands of a skillful salesperson, almost always uncovers a potential opportunity.

Deeper Layers of Truth

I've named one of the most powerful questioning sequences *deeper layers of truth*. Using it effectively is one of the skills that can mark you as a truly outstanding sales performer. It derives its power from the fact that most salespeople are content to interact with their prospects and customers at superficial levels. They never really take the time or the risk to penetrate deeper than the most superficial conversations. As a result, they're left with a cursory understanding of their prospects and shallow relationships with their customers.

Remember the onion graphic from Chapter Eight? That analogy also provides a graphic illustration of the concept of *deeper layers of truth*. Imagine your prospects as being like onions. When you deal with them on the surface, you stay on the edge where it's not too pungent, nor too close to the heart of the matter.

While it's easy and safe to remain on the surface, and interact with people on only the most superficial levels, it also keeps you away from the heart of the issue where the decisions are really made.

However, some salespeople — those who want to excel — develop the ability to penetrate below the surface, to reach the deeper layers of truth. Like cutting into the heart of the onion, they gain the ability to interact with the deeper issues and concerns of their prospects.

Let me illustrate. Suppose you visit a purchasing agent to whom you recently delivered a quote. In the course of the conversation you say something like, "How did we do on that proposal?"

He says, "Not bad, really."

You respond, "Great. When will we know what you're going to do?"

"We think we'll have it resolved soon," he says.

At this point, most salespeople will leave, thinking that they have collected the most pertinent available information. In fact, they have engaged in a very superficial conversation. They have been held to the outer edge of the onion, and haven't penetrated to deeper levels of truth.

Now, it may be true that the salesperson's quotation was not bad. And it may also be true that the prospect thinks they'll have it resolved soon. However, neither one of those replies tell the salesperson anything of value. And they don't give him any information on which to attempt to bring the sale to conclusion.

The top-quality salesperson will not accept these superficial answers, but will instead direct the conversation to deeper levels.

The technique to do so is incredibly simple. Just ask for further clarification and question your prospect's answer. Use questions like "Oh?" or "What do you mean by...?" Let's see how this works.

Back to the same conversation. When your prospect says, "Not bad," you say, "Oh?" and pause to let him speak. The purchasing agent pauses for a moment and responds, "Yes, you were one of the lowest bids." Now, that's a little bit more information. It's just as true as the statement "Not bad," but it's more detailed, more revealing, and therefore, true on a deeper level. But it's not deep enough. So, you respond, "Does that mean you are seriously considering our proposal?"

"Yes."

"And, is low price the only factor on which the business will be awarded?"

"No. There are a number of other things we're considering."

"What are some of those?"

"Well, obviously, we're concerned about the reputation of the supplier, and the ability to meet our specifications and deadlines."

"And how do you feel about our proposal based on those issues?"

"We are a little concerned about your ability to meet our deadlines."

At this point, the salesperson has penetrated to deeper layers of truth, and is talking with the prospect on a level that can make a real difference. In this instance, the conversation has developed almost to the point of negotiation. As the conversation continues, the salesperson will have excellent information on which to make some important decisions. And, he'll understand exactly where the project is at, and what has to be done to manage the sale to fruition.

Compare that to the first salesperson who was content to accept the first, superficial reply. The second salesperson chose to dig for deeper layers of truth by asking "Oh?" and "Why?" questions, and by asking for further or more precise clarification.

This tactic of digging for deeper layers of truth can be used successfully at several points in the sales process.

For example, you can use it when you're probing to discover the prospect's deeper needs and higher priority goals before presenting your product or service.

You may be interviewing a prospect in your first meeting. In response to your answer, he may say, "Yes, we are thinking about upgrading our computer network." Most salespeople will accept that superficially-true answer, and move on from there to say something like,

"Good. Can we make a proposal?"

The salesperson skilled in digging for deeper layers of truth will take the time to understand the prospect more completely and precisely. In so doing, he acquires an edge over his competition because of his deeper knowledge of the prospect. For example, he might say,

"Why are you considering that?"

"What do you hope to gain by the upgrade?"

"What problems are you trying to solve?"

"When, exactly, do you expect to begin and finish this project?"

"Do you have a budget figure in mind?"

Only after digging for deeper layers of truth does the second salesperson move on to the next step in the process. At that point, he has far better information than the first, and is much better equipped to pursue the sale.

At the same time, digging for deeper layers of truth has an additional fringe benefit of causing your prospect to perceive you as competent and professional. As you take the time to intelligently probe the issue, you reveal yourself as a knowledgeable, professional person. The prospect forms his opinion of you based not on what you say, but by what you ask.

In addition, by understanding the prospect more completely and deeply, you become equipped to present a proposal that will more precisely address the deeper concerns of the prospect.

Here are some of the places in the sales process where the deeper layers of truth tactic is most effective:

- In probing for needs and priorities

- To more completely understand a prospect's reactions to presentations and demonstrations.

- At closing, to uncover deeper concerns and objections.

- To more completely understand the personal as opposed to business side of a prospect.

Uncovering deeper layers of truth isn't easy. It requires a salesperson to be skilled in asking questions, to be well-trained, and to have the courage to hang in when the natural reaction is to leave.

Opening the Sale

One of the best applications for well-constructed, appropriately-timed questions is early in the sales process when you're attempting to discover the prospect's Gap.

Often, the sale goes not to the person with the best product or price, but to the one who does the best job of understanding the customer and his situation.

I was asked by one of my clients to work with his sales force. They were having trouble closing the sale. Here's what happened in one sales call I made with them.

We were selling HVAC equipment, and the salesperson had an appointment with the prospect. We met the prospect, and he explained that the building had been expanded several years before, but that nothing had been done to expand the capacity of the air conditioning unit. The company now wanted to do something about that.

The salesperson I worked with asked to see the area in question. He measured the square footage of the room, and then asked to see the existing equipment. We went up into the attic and viewed the existing equipment. There my salesperson estimated the distance from the equipment to the room.

He ended his information collecting by saying to the prospect, "I'll fax you a proposal in a couple days, will that be OK?" The prospect said yes.

At this point, the salesperson had done an adequate job of understanding the technical specifications of the situation, but hadn't even begun to probe into some of the other aspects of the sale. So, I intervened and asked the following questions.

"If you like our proposal, what's the possibility that you'll buy it within the next few weeks?" Here's what he said: "Oh, none at all. I'm just collecting information for budget purposes. We won't actually buy anything until after the new fiscal year in January."

My salesperson didn't know that because he never asked. Instead, he proceeded on the erroneous assumption that the prospect was in a buying mode.

Next I asked about the "situation." I said, "What's your situation? Why is this an issue now?"

He said, "Well, we added space on to this building several years ago. It's always been stuffy in the new part, but we got along OK. At least until last week, when we had a heat wave. The air conditioning had to work so hard that it froze up. So we unplugged it to let the ice thaw. As the ice thawed, it dripped through the ceiling directly onto the president's desk. So, that's why we've decided to do something about it."

Then I said, "What are you looking for in a proposal?"

He said, "Just a ballpark figure we can use for budgeting purposes." I turned to my salesperson and asked, "What's a rough estimate of what it'll take?" He responded, "About $3500."

Then I said, "What can we do to make you look good in this process?"

He said, "I just want to get this off my desk. It's an extra project I don't need right now." I said, "If we get you a ballpark figure, and a set of literature you can show to the boss today, will that help?" He said, "That would be great."

Finally, I asked, "How will a decision be made?" He said, "Around here, the president makes all of those kinds of decisions. So, I'll collect the information and give it to him, and he'll decide what to do from there."

I said, "Could we see him?" The prospect replied, "Would you?" I said, "We'd be happy to." At that point, he set an appointment for us to talk to the president.

The point of all of this is to compare the two different

situations. In the first situation, the salesperson would have vainly spent a lot of time spinning his wheels and then wondering why he didn't close the sale. In the second situation, by the skillful use of questions, we uncovered the truth of the situation, and positioned ourselves to capture the sale.

That's how questions can be used to more completely understand the customer as you open the sale.

Oh?

One of the most powerful and useful questions is the interrogative "Oh?" What happens when you ask someone the question "Oh?" and then pause in silence? Try it. When someone tells you something, say "Oh?" and then be quiet. The person has to jump in and explain. And when they explain, they give you more information, and generally uncover a deeper layer of truth.

As such, "Oh" occupies a special place in the toolbox of an effective distributor salesperson. I believe you can use "Oh" three or four times during the course of a conversation without the person even being aware of it. It's a small and inconspicuous word. And, as soon as you ask it, the person is not thinking about what you just asked, but rather is thinking about what he's going to say in response to it. So "Oh" goes unnoticed.

"Oh" is such a powerful tool because it prompts the other person to explain. And, in the explanation, you acquire powerful information.

Have you seen the movie *Ghost?* If so, you'll remember one of the most poignant scenes in the movie. Demi Moore is working with clay on a potter's wheel — fashioning a pot. The ghost is sitting behind her, with his arms around her. The Righteous

Brothers are singing in the background. We can see the wet clay ooze out between her fingers and run down her arms. It's a sensuous, delicious scene.

Now, focus for a minute on the clay between her hands, the raw material that she's attempting to fashion into a useful thing of beauty.

Like potters working with clay, salespeople are also craftsmen. Only, instead of making pots out of clay, we make sales and relationships out of our customers' responses.

The material that we work with to fashion a sale is the response we get from our customers. With no response, we have nothing to work with, and a sale is virtually impossible. If we're going to be successful craftsmen, and create multiples of sales, then we need to have the material to work with.

The most difficult people to work with are those who don't respond. I still get a tight feeling in my stomach when I recall one of my most memorable failures as a distributor salesperson. I called on one purchasing agent every Tuesday morning for five years, and I was never able to increase my business within that account.

Much of the reason for my failure was my inability to get the purchasing agent to talk. No matter what I did, I could only prompt one-word answers from him.

As a result, I never understood the account like I should have, I never built a relationship with him, and I never increased my business in that account. My failure to sell was a direct result of my failure to gather sufficient "clay" to work with.

Listen Constructively

The primary, but not the only, reason to ask questions is to stimulate the customer to share information with you. If you're not good at accepting and processing that information, you've wasted the effort that you expended to get that far. You need to be a good listener.

It many ways, it's more important to listen well than it is to speak well. Remember the steps in the sales process? It really begins with finding out what your customer wants or needs. That means, when he speaks, you'd better listen and learn to listen well.

I use the words *listen constructively* very intentionally. When you hear the word construction you think of building or assembling something. That's what I mean to imply. It's your job to listen for things to build a relationship upon and to listen for things on which to build a sale.

One of the best techniques involves programming your mind with some questions beforehand. It's a technique borrowed from speed reading. A speed reader first looks through the book's table of contents, and then asks himself questions about the contents. For example, looking through a book on sales techniques, and finding a chapter titled "The Art of Asking Questions," you might ask yourself, "What good is asking questions?" "What applications do they have in sales?" "How can I use questions?"

Once you've loaded those questions into your subconscious mind, as you skim through the words, your mind seeks out the answers to those questions on a level beneath the conscious.

This technique can work for you. Load into your mind the questions you'd like to have answered, and then, as you listen to the customers' responses, your mind searches for the answers to those questions.

Decide what kinds of things you're hoping to hear. Rehearse them in your mind — create a list. For example, you may say to yourself, before you enter into the interaction, "I want to discover some things Bill does that I can connect with — things we have in common. And, I want to find out what the company's position is on this new technology, and if there is anything I can do to influence the proposal I made last month that doesn't seem to be getting anywhere."

Now, translate each of those objectives into questions. Your list could then look like this:

"What do I have in common with Bill?"

"What is their position on the new technology?"

"What is their position on my last proposal?

"What would they like to see me change in my proposal in order to get the business?"

At this point, you've loaded into your mind the questions that you can use to construct a more solid relationship and to build a sale. You're prepared to listen constructively.

Listen and observe more than just words. Listen to the choices of subjects your customer makes. The things that he chooses to talk about are the things that are the most important to him.

Listen to what is *not* being said. Sometimes people will intentionally talk around a subject that is too emotionally charged for them. For example, a customer may not want to mention the problems he's having with his current supplier if that supplier was his choice. To admit to the problems would be to admit to his mistake.

Finally, notice your prospect's body language. It can reveal a whole dimension of attitudes and feelings that you may not understand any other way.

Seven Listening Mistakes

1. Don't do all the talking. Too many salespeople talk themselves out of sales by talking too much. Remember the scene from *Ghost.* The material that you use to create a sale is not *your* conversation, it's your customer's conversation. If you're talking, your customer is not.

2. Don't interrupt when others are talking. First, it's rude. Second, it's unwise. If you interrupt your customer before he's finished, you may never know the things that he was in the process of telling you. That's a bit of clay for your craftsmanship that you'll never have.

3. Don't start to argue or take exception before the person has finished. This can be incredibly hard at times. But it's just a variation of the previous rule. It doesn't serve you well to interrupt your customer. It's always better to let him finish.

4. Don't digress with a personal story all the time. There are times to tell a personal story. It's a good way to connect with your customer, particularly early in a relationship. But it can get tedious if you do it all the time, *and*, you can waste time and divert the conversation if you do it too much.

5. Don't finish sentences for people. Again, it's rude, and it causes frustration on the part of your customer.

6. Don't wait impatiently for someone to finish so you can interject. Generally, the person speaking notices your impatience. That can be disconcerting to your customer. If you're fidgeting impatiently while you wait, both you and your customer know that you're not listening to him — you're thinking about what you want to say in response. You can't listen while you're thinking about your comeback.

7. Don't work too hard at maintaining eye contact. You'll make people uncomfortable if you use unrelenting eye contact. You need to look away regularly to relieve the tension.

Respond positively

You're not finished when you listen constructively. To be good at asking questions, you need to respond positively to every answer you receive. The sequence isn't ask a question, listen to the answer, and then ask the next question. Instead, it is ask a question, listen to the response, respond to the answer, then ask another question.

Your ability to continue to maintain an atmosphere that encourages your customer to answer additional questions rests, in large measure, on your skill in responding positively. Getting your customer to continue to answer questions is an absolute necessity for you to successfully construct a sale.

Respond to everything. Every time your customer answers one of your questions, respond to that answer. Make sure that you respond to their answers positively.

You can use body language, like a nod of the head, or a facial expression, like a smile. The important thing is that your customer understands that you have heard and accepted what he has said.

Paraphrasing what your customer says, and feeding it back to him, is a powerful response. Asking a thoughtful question about his answer is another. If nothing else, you can use verbal reinforcers like , "thanks," "really," and "oh" as a response, not as an interrogative.

Making the Most of Your Strategic Advantage

The days will soon be gone when you can make a good living picking up orders, visiting with old friends, and selling product or price. If you're going to excel at distributor sales, you must also find ways to sell contracts, systems and multi-product line deals. That begins with the systematic penetration of your key accounts and knowing your highest potential customers more broadly and deeply than your competitors do.

Let's put our knowledge to use in forming a comprehensive sales strategy. The strategy is this: Use your frequent customer contacts to know your customer more deeply, more broadly, and in a more detailed fashion than your competitors. This knowledge of the customer will result in greater opportunities for you by empowering you to bring creative, unique proposals to solve their deeper needs. And that's what will distinguish you from the competition.

Implement your strategy at two levels. First, implement it at the account level. Focus on knowing your accounts, particularly your A accounts, in a broader, deeper and more detailed way.

"Broader" means expanding your contacts and relationships horizontally within your key accounts. Make it a point to systematically meet all the department heads, engineers, and supervisors. Then use your questioning skills to learn about their systematic problems and goals. Don't think of selling just product, but rather begin to think of yourself as a problem solver, able to help your key accounts with systematic solutions to multi-department problems.

As you extend your influence and knowledge more broadly within the account, work at extending it deeper. Work to meet and know key players up the hierarchy. Know your primary contact's boss, and know his boss. Meet the CFO and CEO if you can. Talk to these higher-ups about systematic solutions.

Use the account profiles and your newly enhanced skill in asking questions to capture useful marketing information.

I learned a lesson about the power of extending my relationships more deeply the hard way. As a distributor rep, I initially spent most of my time calling on purchasing agents and department heads. It never occurred to me to try to meet and get to know their bosses. One day, one of my best accounts announced they could no longer do business with me. It seems that my primary competitor had signed a prime vendor contract with the hospital. While I was calling on the grass roots people, he was calling on their bosses — the CFO and administrative people. He was able to present them with a solution designed to reduce their costs of acquisition and storage. The hospital bought it, and I was out.

As you focus on extending your relationships and knowledge deeply and broadly on the account level, apply the same strategy on an individual level.

First, concentrate on knowing the individuals within your accounts better. If you're going to know your customer better, you must ask deeper and more detailed questions. Use the customer profile forms as a tool to help you.

Putting these skills together into a consistent strategy will provide you with the basis for the advantage you need to excel.

To implement the ideas in this chapter...

1. Prepare a set of questions for each of the most common sales situations you find yourself in.

2. Be sensitive to the emotional atmosphere surrounding your interactions with your customers, and work to create a feeling of comfort and honesty.

3. Practice the *deeper layers of truth* technique.

4. Create some questions that specifically help open the sale and uncover the customer's Gap.

5. Regularly work the question "Oh?" into your conversations.

6. Practice programming your mind with questions as a listening technique.

7. Make it a rule to respond to every answer you receive in response to your question.

Chapter Eleven
Transferable Sales Skills — Part Four: Closing the Sale

Back to our baseball diamond analogy. You've created some comfort and rapport with your prospect — that's getting to the batter's box. Then, through the skillful use of questions and constructive listening, you have understood the prospect's Gap. Congratulations. It is these two steps, and your ability to execute them skillfully and effectively, that distinguish the excellent salespeople from the mediocre.

But, although you may have skillfully gotten to first base and distinguished yourself from your competition in that aspect, you still need to complete the run around the bases to score. Second and third bases are next, and that means describing to the customer the reasons why he should purchase your product or program.

Regardless of what you're selling — whether it's the latest widget, a new service, or a systems contract — you'll still need to persuasively describe the details of the proposal to your prospect. That means describing the features and benefits of your offering.

You're familiar with features. They are the describable characteristics of your product. Features are the answers to questions like this: "What is it?,"

"What does it do?," "How does it do it?," "What is it made of?," and "How is it different?"

For example, if you're presenting a product, let's say a green widget, the features are the describable characteristics of that widget. You could say that it is made of steel, painted green, shaped a certain way, comes in boxes of 12, and is manufactured in the United States. All of these are features of the product.

If you're selling a systems contract, that offering also has features. It might be the delivery rates, numbers of deliveries per week or month, guaranteed fill rates, number of times you'll visit the customer, etc.

Not only does the product offering that you present to your prospect have features, but so do the other aspects of the total decision to buy. Your company has features, the terms have features, the service you provide has features, and you have features!

In fact, if you added up all the features you have to talk about, you'd find that you can't possibly mention everything. Which brings us to one principle of presenting features and benefits. Only present those features that relate directly to the customer's Gap.

Most salespeople say too much. They often talk themselves out of a sale by assuming a customer is interested in some feature, mentioning and stressing that feature which may turn out to be a negative in the prospect's mind. Once you plant a negative in your prospect's mind, it is very difficult to remove it.

Here's an example. Let's say you're presenting a set of marking pens to your prospect in response to his need for a means of writing on transparencies. You mention that the pens can be purchased in sets of eight different colors. And, although you don't mention it, the pens can also be purchased individually in the color of your choice. You assumed, however, that the prospect would want a selection of colors, and chose to present only that feature. But what if your prospect is color blind? The possibility of dealing with a set of eight different colors where he is unable to distinguish one pen from another presents him with an uneasy negative. You did that — you inserted in his mind a negative by assuming that he was interested in some feature when that wasn't the case.

The moral of this story is to make sure you choose those features that are right for each prospect. Relate each feature you mention to a specific need or interest expressed or implied by the prospect.

Once you have described a feature, you've safely negotiated second base. Now it's time to move to third.

This step requires you to translate features into benefits. A benefit is a statement that describes what the features mean to the prospect. It answers questions like "So what?", and "What's in it for me?"

Here's an easy-to-remember way to translate features into benefits. Use the transitional phrase, "This means that you...." For example, you may say, "Our green widgets are made in the United States." That's a feature. Imagine your prospect silently voicing the question, "So what?" You say, "This means that you can be sure that replacement parts are readily available."

Notice that, when you describe the benefit, the subject of your sentence changes. You are no longer talking about your product, instead you're talking about the other person. People don't buy features, they buy what the features do for them. And what the features do for them is called a benefit. No presentation is complete without your best attempt to translate all the features into clear and compelling benefits.

Once you complete this step, you've reached third base. At this point, how many runs have you scored? Obviously, the answer is none. Nothing really counts until you have crossed home plate, and that means closing the sale.

Closing the Sale

Whenever I ask distributor salespeople to rate themselves on their competence at all the different parts of the sales process, they invariably rate themselves low at closing the sale.

There are a couple of reasons for this. In the past, most distributor sales had a very high component of service to the job. And the people hired to be distributor salespeople often came from a service background. Their personality, training, and experience all combined to detract from their perception of themselves as closers. At the same time, because of the high relationship aspects of the distributor sales process, many distributor salespeople have been hesitant to improve their closing skills for fear that it might jeopardize customer relationships.

That is changing, however, as the need for salespeople to become more productive and effective grows. Salespeople who don't resolve the issue and get a decision from the customer waste time. And there is no time to be wasted in the new environment.

So, let's examine the issue of closing. The first step is to understand what a close is. I like to define it broadly by offering two definitions:

- Closing is acquiring an agreement on the part of your prospect or customer to take action.

- Closing is bringing an issue to resolution.

Understood that way, closing is not just asking for an order. Rather, it is something that you do over and over, at every stage of the sales process. In fact, almost every time you interact with a prospect or customer, you can close the interaction by asking for some agreement.

Let's apply the definition to a real life situation. Suppose you're talking on the phone to a prospect, and he says, "Sounds interesting. Send me some literature." You say, "OK, I'll put it in the mail today." Have you closed?

The answer is no. You have agreed to take action — send some literature — but your prospect hasn't agreed to do anything. Can you turn the same situation into a close?

Here's how to do it. Back to the same situation. Your prospect says, "Sounds interesting. Send me some literature." You remark, "I'd be happy to. After you review it, will you discuss it with me over the phone, say next Friday?" If your prospect says, "Yes," you've closed. He's agreed to take some action.

Understanding that definition is crucial to closing the sale for a distributor sales rep. Many of the offers and proposals you work on are very involved, requiring a number of steps in the analysis and decision making for your customer. By continuing to ask for some kind of action, you keep the project moving forward. The final decision to buy is often made when you're not there. It is often the natural, local consequence of the decisions that lead up to it.

That leads us to a powerful principle of closing the sale for distributor reps: Close every interaction. In other words, at the conclusion of *every* interaction with your customer, ask for an agreement on the action he'll take.

The telephone conversation described above is a good example of closing the interaction. Here's another common situation. Let's say you've discussed a product or proposal with your customer. He says, "It looks interesting, but we're not ready for that now." You might then say, "When do you think will be a good time?" Your customer responds, "Probably around June." You might typically say, "OK, I'll make a note to discuss it with you then." At this point, you haven't closed the interaction, nor have you resolved the issue.

Let's take the conversation one more step further. Suppose you now say, "At that point in time, will you spend an hour with me to discuss it in detail?" You have now attempted to close the interaction by getting an agreement for action on the part of your customer. You've put the issue on the table, and are attempting to resolve it.

Let's take the conversation one step further. Suppose your customer says, "No, probably not." You now have a decision to make. Should you probe the reasons why, or should you accept his decision? Let's say you decide to accept his decision. The conversation has value to it in that you learned that this proposal isn't going to fly in this account. The early "no" was valuable to you. You didn't waste months chasing something that wasn't going to happen. That's the value in resolving the issue.

Let's now say that your prospect, instead of responding "no," responds to your close by saying, "Yeah, I think it has enough merit to spend that time discussing it with you." You now have his commitment to spend an hour with you, so you have moved the issue forward. You're one step closer to the ultimate sale.

Implement these two concepts and you'll dramatically improve your productivity. Keep in mind that closing is asking for agreement and bringing the issue to resolution. Make it your goal to close every interaction.

The Dynamics of the Closing Process

Let's take closing one step deeper by considering the dynamics of the closing process. What happens when you ask for agreement? Illustration # 12 flowcharts the process. It begins when you ask your customer to take action. That's the close.

The Dynamics of the Closing Process

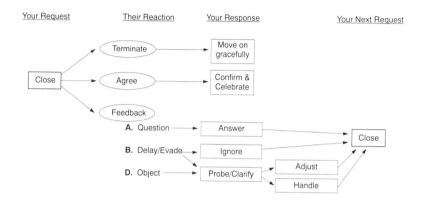

Illustration #12

Your prospect then reacts to your request. There are only a limited number of ways in which your customer can react. He can terminate the conversation by telling you definitely, absolutely, without question, "NO!" I call that the *terminal no.*

It's very important for you to be able to distinguish a terminal no from a *tentative* no. A tentative no is when the customer says "no", but really means something like, "Probably not," or "Maybe."

I recall one of my most memorable illustrations of this principle. I was visiting, for the first time, one of the hospitals assigned to me. I was able to meet with the material manager, a crusty older man who delighted in making salespeople squirm. I did my introductory pitch to him, and he responded with this comment: "Young man, we have too many vendors right now. We're trying to reduce the number of vendors we have. So we're not interested in dealing with someone new. Secondly, we don't know much about your company. But what we do know, we don't like. So, I'd advise you to not waste your time here."

I interpreted that as a tentative no, not a terminal no. Several weeks later I went back to see him again. This time, I thought I'd play my strongest card by presenting a product which almost every hospital in the state bought from us — suction tubing. Suction tubing is a staple item in a hospital, and is used by every hospital in a number of different departments. At the time, we had an arrangement with the premier manufacturer guaranteeing us the best prices in the state. Almost every other hospital bought it from us. I was sure he had to buy my suction tubing deal.

After I presented it to him, he sighed and said, "We don't use any." I turned in my chair and looked into the hallway outside his office. There was a cart with some suction tubing hanging from it. Telling me they didn't use suction tubing was like saying they have no beds in their hospital. He was lying — I knew it and he knew it.

I chose to interpret that as a tentative no, not a terminal no. As luck would have it, several months later, I was able to find a buyer in the hospital who I could work with. I discovered a tiny opening when one of their current suppliers messed up, and I was given an opportunity to bring in a product. We did well with that line, and one thing led to another. Within three years, that account had grown so much that it became the hospital for which I had the greatest penetration of all my accounts.

All because I was able to distinguish between a tentative no and a terminal no.

If your prospect doesn't terminate, he can agree to the action you've suggested.

Another possibility is that he doesn't say either yes or no, but instead gives you some feedback. By definition, your prospect can only do one of three things: terminate, agree, or provide feedback.

There are three kinds of feedback that your customers can provide. By definition, every possible word out of their mouths will fit into one of these three categories: question, evasion, or objection.

You know what a question is. An evasion is when your prospect makes a comment that suggests he isn't willing to commit himself to any position. The classic, "I want to think about it," is an example. An objection is a reason for not doing what you want your prospect to do.

Once your prospect has reacted, it's time for you to respond to his reaction. Let's think about each of these possibilities. If he terminates, what is your most appropriate response? Move on gracefully. Don't get angry, don't slam the door or call him names. You never know when that person will surface again at some other account. Move on gracefully, remembering the first law of sales: You don't sell them all.

If he agrees, confirm the agreement and then celebrate! Good for you, you got one. Enjoy the burst of pleasure that gives you. It's one of the reasons you're a salesperson. There is a certain satisfaction and a high that comes from getting agreement, especially on a big deal, that is a special fringe benefit of selling.

Let's look at feedback. If your prospect asks you a question, what do you do? Answer the question. That's simple enough. If he evades your question, you have two appropriate choices.

The first is to ignore his evasive comment. That's right, ignore it. I remember hearing a sales trainer some years ago talk about ignoring a prospect's first evasion. He said that, the first time someone offers you an evasion, they are merely processing the issue in their mind, and don't really mean what they said. So, it's often best to ignore it and go on.

Let's say you ask the question, "Should we go ahead with this?" And your prospect says, "I'd like to think about it a little." Your response is, "Should we deliver it Monday, or is Tuesday better?" You've totally ignored their comment.

I have found this technique works once — for their first evasion. But don't do it more than once in an interaction.

Your other choice is to probe or clarify your customer's position. Probing and clarifying is always the best immediate response to an evasion or objection of any kind.

This process requires a three-step approach. Here's how you do it.

1. Empathize. Begin by empathizing with your customer. That takes some of the tension out of the situation, defuses any defensiveness on his part, and builds a positive atmosphere. Empathizing requires you to do two things. First, make a statement indicating that you understand how the prospect thinks or feels. Second, support that statement with some proof.

Here's an example. Let's say your prospect has said, "I want to think it over." You respond by empathizing. You say, "I know how you feel," (that's your empathizing statement). "Many of my other customers responded the same way when they were first presented with this concept," (that's your proof). Your proof is the reason they should believe that you really do understand how they think or feel.

2. Question. Once you've empathized with your prospect, then question him. Generally, when you're responding to an objection or evasion, the issue is too general to deal with adequately. Often your prospect hasn't accurately articulated the thoughts in his own mind. Your questions should therefore be of the type that require your prospect to think more specifically. You must take his answer from the vague and general to the specific. You can't respond to a vague comment, but you can respond to a specific one. The primary tool for moving your prospect from general to specific thoughts is a good question.

Back to our example. After you've empathized, next ask, "When you say that you want to think about it, what specifically is it that you need to consider more deeply?" Notice the question asks the prospect to think more specifically — to move from the general to the specific.

3. Verify. When he answers, you then rephrase the answer and feed it back to him, confirming that it really is the way he thinks or feels. Back to the example. Let's say he says, "Well, John, I'm not sure about the price. It's more than we had planned in the budget. I'm not sure we want to pay that much." That would be a great answer, because it reveals the specific issue that is bothering the prospect.

Your skillful empathizing and questioning has uncovered the real problem. Now, you just rephrase it and ask for him to confirm what you've said. Your response could go like this. "OK. So, in other words, you're concerned about how you can pay for it when it's more than what you had budgeted. Is that right?" When your prospect confirms it, you have successfully probed and clarified his evasion or objection to the point where you've moved from the general to the specific. Now, you can deal with it.

As long as he maintains that he "just wants to think about it," there is little you can do to move the project forward. But now that you understand exactly what the issue is, you can respond to the objection.

OK, you've clarified your prospect's evasion or objection to the point that it's a specific, understandable issue. Now what?

You can do one of two things. Your first option is to adjust your proposal or presentation to your improved understanding of your prospect's situation and perception. In other words, you change. If your prospect says, "It's two dollars too much," then you have the choice of saying, "OK, for you, we'll drop the price by two dollars." You've changed your proposal to meet your revised understanding of your prospect.

Your second option is to respond to the objection in such a way so as to influence your prospect to change. That means that you must get him to think differently.

How you do this can vary tremendously by the type of objection your prospect has raised. There are an unlimited number of objections, and an unlimited number of ways to respond to them. Rather than attempt to identify a hundred different strategies, I'd prefer to show you a process you can use to create your own responses.

The secret is to *prepare* for your most likely objections. Here's how to do it.

- Identify the five or six most common objections you hear.

- Think about each one of them. Think about them in very specific, disciplined ways. Do two things.

  - Prepare a flow chart of the way in which you want to respond to that objection.

  - Prepare the language and ammunition you'll need to support your position.

Here's an example. Let's say your prospect says, after you have probed and clarified his first response, "It costs too much."

As you think about responding to this objection, you decide that the first thing you're going to do is empathize once again.

So, you draw a box on your flow chart and write in "Empathize." Then what? You decide you need to find out how much is too much. So, you draw another box underneath the first, and write in it, "Ask how much is too much." Next, you decide to restate the benefits of your proposal to the customer. So, you draw the next box under that and write in it, "Restate the benefits." Then you decide to translate the too much amount into the smallest way of expressing it. In other words, if it's $500 too much, and that is for a year-long time period, then it's really only about $1.35 a day too much. So, draw another box and write in it, "Translate into lowest expression." Next, compare the benefits to that low expression. So write in the next box, "Compare benefits to lowest expression." Finally, you decide to close again — that goes into your last box.

Now, what you have is a flow chart of the steps you want to follow when you hear this objection. But you're not finished yet. Collect whatever ammunition you can find to support your statements. For example, do you have any third party studies that confirm the benefits you've described? Any testimonials, articles from trade journals, etc.? Gather that kind of documentation, and have it in your briefcase ready to use when you meet your prospect's objections.

That brings us to the last column in Illustration #10, "Close again." That starts the whole process all over again.

Team Decisions

How do you close the sale when the decision is made by a team or committee, and you can't be there when they make the decision?

This situation is growing more and more common as the trend towards Total Quality Management programs spreads, and teams do more of the decision making that was previously the job of individuals. In closing this situation, I'm going to first assume that you've done a thorough job of selling. In other words, you have reached all the available team members, talked with them individually, understood their Gap, and made a coherent, powerful presentation of your best solution to their problems. If you haven't done that, then you need to do it first, before you attempt to bring the issue to closure.

Now, let's say that you have finished selling, and the team is going to make a decision. What do you do? Here's the most effective approach. Find the team member who you think is most strongly in favor of your solution, and ask him or her to advocate it to the team. Your request for action is not, "Will you buy this?" Rather, the issue you put before that team member is, "Will you recommend this?"

If you can get one strong team member who is on your side and willing to argue for you, your chances of closing that sale will be dramatically enhanced.

Alternate Next Steps

Much of the literature about closing works on the assumption that the person to whom you're speaking is the decision maker, and that he has the authority to make the decision while you're there with them. However, this situation is growing increasingly less frequent. Many organizations are adopting policies and procedures which require multiple sign-offs on a decision and/or team approaches. In such cases, it's inappropriate for you to ask for the order when your prospect does not have the appropriate authority.

In this situation, it's important that you develop alternate next steps. While you may want the purchase order, your buyer may not be able to give it to you for reasons that are totally beyond your ability to influence. Your best strategy is to back off, and ask for something that isn't quite as difficult. I call that *preparing an alternate next step.*

Here's an example. I once had a CPA firm as a client. The firm wanted to acquire additional customers for its computerized bookkeeping service. We developed a sales and marketing system which put them in front of a number of qualified prospects. At the first sales call, they asked the prospect to sign up for their bookkeeping service.

Think back to the discussion of risk and relationship from Chapter Six. Giving someone your bookkeeping business is a high risk decision. Few prospects were ready to do that on the strength of just one sales call. So, when it became apparent that someone was not going to say yes to the major proposal, they were prepared with a fall-back position. The fall-back position was to ask the prospect for a set of his financial statements, so that the CPA firm could prepare an example of what the computerized report would look like, using the prospect's own figures.

Notice that this alternate next step kept the proposal alive and moving forward while at the same time recognizing that some people were legitimately not ready to say yes to the big deal.

That's an example of an alternate next step. One of the best ways to prepare for closing is to think through each of your closing situations, and to prepare one or two alternate next steps that allow your prospect or customer to say yes to you and keep the project moving forward.

To implement the ideas in this chapter...

1. Focus on translating the features of your products and programs into benefits for the customer.

2. Set a goal to end every interaction with an agreement.

3. Keep the dynamics of the closing process in mind at every closing opportunity.

4. Practice the three step clarifying approach when faced with an objection.

5. Before presenting your next proposal, prepare for the most common objections.

6. Create alternate next steps for every team decision.

Chapter Twelve
Controlling Yourself —
Part One: Take Charge of
Your Attitude

It's long been my belief that only half of a salesperson's challenge is working with other people. That's the part that gets the most press, and the portion that many salespeople are most interested in.

But, if you're going to be an effective salesperson — an excellent distributor salesperson — you need to gain mastery over the other half of your job. That means gaining mastery of yourself. If you can learn to control yourself, you'll eventually learn to do everything else.

Gaining control of yourself means learning to get the most out of yourself by harnessing your skills and energy to their most productive purposes. Some of the strategies you'll need to implement in order to do so include: mastering goal setting; learning how to change your habits; controlling your emotions; dealing successfully with adversity and failure; overcoming procrastination and fear; and changing your underlying beliefs about the world and yourself.

Sounds awesome, and it is. The greatest challenge for any salesperson is the internal struggle to gain control of yourself.

Let's begin by looking at how all this works together to affect your sales performance.

Sales Success from the Inside Out

Look at Illustration #13. It's back to our onion analogy again. Only this time the onion is you. The layers of onion represent levels of depth in you. On the very surface are your interactions with other people. Those are often shaped and directed by the sales tactics we've been talking about. This is the you that your customers see. It's the most superficial part of you.

As we peel each layer off of the onion, we go deeper into the person that you are. Just beneath the surface are the strategies you design, the goals you set, the habits you have built up over the years, and the ways you go about doing things.

For example, let's say you ask your customer good questions. That's a tactic — on the very surface of your being. It's where you interact with someone else.

The reason you ask questions — the motivating force that underlies your use of that tactic — can be one of a number of things. Perhaps it arises out of a strategic plan you created to learn more about your customer.

Or, you may have developed a goal to ask four questions during the course of the day. Maybe it's just your habit to always ask good questions. Finally, it could be a process that you've created that requires you to fill out a form with the answer to that question.

Your sales behavior always arises out of one of those four motivations. You either work intentionally, with planning and forethought, as evidenced by your goals and strategies, or you

Changing From the Inside Out

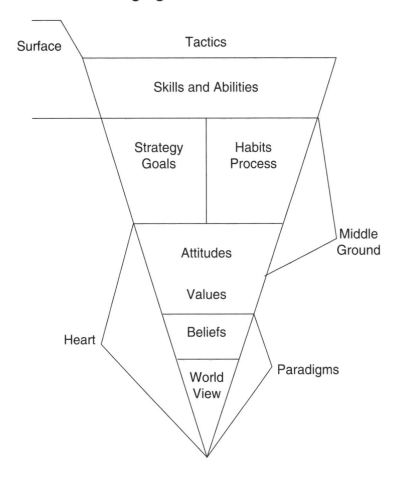

Illustration #13

work "unconsciously," through your habits and routines. These motivating forces lie just beneath the surface.

Peel off that layer of the onion, and you'll find, at the next deepest level, your attitudes. You've heard many times about the importance of a good attitude. That's because your attitudes give rise to your habits and your goals.

When you're burdened with a depressed, pessimistic attitude, you don't set worthwhile goals or aspire to great accomplishment. The opposite is also true. When you have positive, optimistic attitudes, you naturally aspire to challenging goals, and that leads to energy and positive behavior.

If your attitude is positive, you'll feel like you can positively influence a prospect. That positive attitude can lead you to creating a goal and developing the strategy that you'll need to achieve that goal.

Back to the asking questions example. Let's say your positive attitude has led you to develop the goal of acquiring three new accounts this month. Now that you're optimistic enough to set a challenging goal, you need to create a strategy to achieve it. So, you decide on a strategy, part of which requires you to ask good questions of a certain number of prospects.

In this example, your attitude led to the vision of a goal, which led to a strategy, which led to the actions you took with your prospect. *Your actions bubbled up from the inside out.*

But, you're still not at the very heart of things. Underlying your attitudes are your values. Values refer to the things you hold dear and important. For example, you may value integrity, success in your job, and your spouse very highly. These values give rise to certain attitudes about those things.

Take the situation where you highly value your spouse and his or her physical well-being. Since you value him or her so highly, you think positively about your ability to provide protection and security. Out of that attitude arises your goals and strategies.

But, you're still not finished. Underlying and supporting your values are your beliefs. For example, you may believe that it is always the husband's responsibility to support the family no matter what. This belief may be so deep inside you that you never really articulated it. It's just been embedded deep into your psyche.

As a result of that belief, you place a high value on the physical well-being of your spouse because, after all, it's your job to take care of that. That value leads to attitudes, which lead to goals or habits, which lead to behavior.

There is yet one layer deeper, the heart of the onion. And that is your worldview. Your worldview is comprised of your fundamental, core beliefs about the world and yourself. It's composed of the absolute deepest beliefs you hold about your purpose in life and the way in which the world functions. It differs from the beliefs above it only in degree. The worldview comprises the beginning of the spiritual part of ourselves. These beliefs shape everything above them.

For example, one person may believe that the universe is so connected that everything we do is a result of fate or destiny. Another individual may believe the opposite, that we are creatures with free will existing in a world that responds to us. A third may believe that we are the creation of a loving God — designed for a specific purpose.

This basic view of yourself and the world is usually influenced by your culture. It is often influenced by religious education, because it borders on the spiritual part of us.

Now, you're probably wondering what all this has to do with sales. Study the illustration. Notice that there is a direct relationship between the higher layers and the deeper layers.

When changes are made in the deeper layers, those changes affect everything above them. Because of the nature of the pie-shape illustration, a small change deep down in a person will affect a great deal of things above it.

If you change your attitudes, you'll change your strategy, habits and actions. Change your values and your beliefs, and you can't help but change your attitudes. Modify your worldview, and everything above it will change.

If you believe that one of your challenges is to continually improve yourself, to constantly change your behavior in positive ways, then the deeper you make those changes, the broader and more powerful will be the changes on the surface.

One way, then, to control yourself and harness your energies and abilities in the most positive ways is to carefully consider your deeper layers. Challenge your values, examine your beliefs, resolve the question of your purpose in life. I once taught an intense 10 week sales training program in which the first week was given to a discussion of world-views, and the first assignment was to write a statement of your purpose in life.

Why bother? Because the more completely you resolve the deeper issues, the more likely it will be that you will have congruence, not conflict in all the layers above. I have never met a consistently successful professional salesperson who hadn't calmly and confidently resolved the deeper issues. I have met hundreds of salespeople who have had short-term success, sometimes spectacularly so, but whose lack of deeper grounding spun them out of control, crashing and burning in some self-defeating behavior.

To make significant, long-lasting, permanent changes in your results, resolve the deeper issues in your life.

Dealing with Failure

Probably the most common experience a salesperson has is failure. Think about it. You probably make less than 50 percent of the appointments you attempt to make. So, most of the time, you fail. You probably sell less than 50 percent of the proposals or demonstrations you make. See what I mean? You're like a baseball player who is only successful at bat a third of the time. It's not the success that gets to us mentally, it's the failures.

So, dealing with failure is one of those skills that is rarely talked about, but absolutely essential to the success of a distributor salesperson.

In my life, I certainly remember my failures more clearly than I do my successes. At one point in my sales career, I sold capital equipment. Specifically, amplification equipment for classrooms of hearing impaired children. These systems were sold to the special education school systems, and were budgeted, big- ticket items.

In one year, there were 29 deals available in my territory. Of those 29, I got 28 orders. But ask me which one I remember most clearly and which one I learned the most from. You know it — my one failure.

Adversity is like failure in that it produces a negative situation for us. The difference is that adversity is not always your own doing. Sometimes it falls on you without any direct involvement of your part. It hits all of us, not just distributor salespeople. However, because salespeople live with failure and rejection so often, you're more susceptible to the negative consequences of adversity. It's easy to get depressed and down on yourself when you fail if, at the same time, you're struggling with some kind of adversity.

One of my greatest challenges as a salesperson occurred a

few years before I entered distributor sales. I had decided to leave the amplification equipment company, and accepted a position selling surgical staplers.

This was a major risk on my part. I was the number one salesperson in the nation for my current employer, had a good salary, a company car, and great prospects. However, I was bored and looking for another challenge. So I accepted a position which was the opposite in many ways — I earned straight commission and had to buy my own demonstration samples from the company.

However, before I accepted the offer, I calculated the amount of business that was in existence in the territory. I felt that, if I could double the business within the first year, I'd be OK. After that, any sales increases would bring about real increases in my standard of living.

So I took the plunge and went off to New York for six weeks of intense training. While I was gone, the district sales managers changed. When I returned home from training, I was quickly met by my new district sales manger, who announced that he had changed my territory. The territory that I was hired for wasn't the territory I was going to get. In fact, the territory I ended up with had only about 30 percent of the existing business I was counting on.

I was outraged. How could they do this to me? What kind of a company was this that would treat its employees that way? I immediately decided that I didn't want to work for them and began looking for a different job. However, it only took a few weeks for me to realize that I was seen as unemployable. Most people I interviewed with saw my quick desire to leave as a weakness in me, not my company.

One thing led to another and, after six months, I owed the company $10,000 (a lot of money in the mid '70s), my draw was finished, and I had few prospects for finding another job. Talk about being between a rock and a hard place!

That was adversity, compounded by my failure to effectively sell the product.

How do you deal with failure and adversity? Here are several suggestions from my experience and study.

1. Accept the new reality. No use moping about it. No use pretending that it'll go away or change or that it doesn't matter. It *does* matter or else you wouldn't be thinking about it. Accept that you failed. Accept that your situation is not what you'd like it to be. Once you accept it, and stop denying it or fighting it, you can go on from there.

At the same time that you accept the new reality, accept your responsibility to do something about it. No one is going to bail you out. The reality is that you're in this situation, and *you* need to do something about it.

When I finally saw, in a moment of blinding clarity, that my situation was pretty much my own doing, it was like a great weight off my shoulders. I now had the power to do something about it! I was once again in a situation where I could influence the world around me and affect my life. It wasn't them, it was me!

And since it was me, the power to do something was also in me!

2. Ask Questions. This is a great time to learn. Remember, you'll generally learn more from your failures than you will from your successes, providing that you're ready and able to learn. The first step in the learning process is to reflect back on what happened and ask questions about it. How did it happen? Why? What did you do (not do) to bring this situation about? What could you have done differently? How did your customer react? How did your competitor act? Is there some lesson in that?

Got the idea? Begin with questions.

In my situation, my question asking routine led me to the conclusion that my bitterness and negativity was the major problem. If I could do away with that, I could be more effective.

3. Draw conclusions. Once you ask the questions, answer them fully. After each question you ask about the situation, follow it with this question that you ask about yourself: "What should I do differently in the future?"

If you ask, "What did I do to create this situation?" and your answer is, "I didn't thoroughly prepare my presentation," then ask the second question, "What should I do differently in the future?" The answer to that question is your conclusion: "I should make sure I am thoroughly prepared for every presentation."

These conclusions, or reflections on life and your behavior, are the single most important fruits of your failure. Almost any failure is worthwhile if it stimulates some changed behavior and deeper understanding on your part. It's not what happens that's important in the long run — it's what you learn from it that counts.

In my situation, I concluded that I needed to stimulate myself to be positive. And to overcome my bitterness and resentment with positive self-confidence.

4. Play with situations. Start little what-if games in your imagination. If you're in a miserable situation, begin by asking yourself: "What if I did this....?" "What if I did that...?" See if this doesn't stimulate some creative, exciting possibilities for you.

I asked myself how I could overcome my internal bitterness and resentment. I did the "what-if" games and came up with a novel approach. I decided that I needed to change my attitudes. I was caught in a negative mode, and I needed to change that to a positive mode. I reasoned that I needed to put into my head positive, confident thoughts.

At the time, I was living on the outskirts of my territory, and I had a daily 35 minute drive into the metropolitan Detroit area on Interstate 96. I decided to make use of that 35 minutes every morning to put positive thoughts into my head.

I spent an evening finding all the powerful, positive promises in the Bible, and wrote them on 3" X 5" cards. Then, each morning, I'd hold the 3" X 5" cards in front of me on the steering wheel, and flip through them over and over — reading them repetitively as I drove into the city.

5. Focus on short-term possibilities. When life seems to have dealt you the most unfair blow, and the future looks miserable, stop contemplating the future. It's no fun thinking about how miserable you're going to be. Instead, focus on the short-term possibilities.

I'm a great believer in long-term goals. But I also have been through enough miserable situations in my life to know that there are times when it's best to forget (for now) those long-term goals and focus on the positive things you can do today!

I can't tell you how many time in my life I've found this discipline to be a powerful tonic to a depressed view of the future. Instead of thinking about next year, think about tomorrow. What positive things can you do tomorrow? Or, better yet, today. What's the single most positive thing you can do today? Give yourself realistic, short terms goals. And, I mean *really* short term — today and tomorrow. Think in terms of positive actions. You may not be able to create any long-term or mid-term goals in your current state of mind, but you still have the ability to select right from wrong, good from bad, and positive from negative. So, focus on the very short term. Do the most positive things you can think of to do today, and don't worry about long-term goals.

Back to my situation. With no draw, no commissions, no salary, and lots of financial responsibilities, I couldn't think in terms of my long-term financial goals. I decided to focus on today and tomorrow, and do the best things I could do short term. Instead of thinking about developing some account next month, I'd visit it today. I discovered a discipline I turned into a habit which was to serve me well from then on. Several times during the course of the day, I'd ask myself, "Am I doing the thing that is the single most effective thing for me to be doing right now?" If the answer was "no," I would change what I was doing.

At the same time, I remember deciding that, outside of my working day, the single most positive thing I could do was exercise. It always made me feel better. I knew it to be a good thing. So I began an exercise program.

Were these two things strategically designed to meet some long-term goal of mine? No! Were they my best response to the need to do something positive every day? You bet!

In neither case was I focused on long-term goals. However, I wasn't in the kind of circumstance where I felt long-term goals were possible. I couldn't see how I was going to survive my current mess. So, I focused on the very short-term positive things I could do today.

When I was squarely in the middle of the rock and hard place trying to sell surgical staplers, I couldn't imagine paying off that $10,000 debt. So I didn't think about it. Instead, I focused on using each day in the most positive way I could.

6. Act. Sooner or later, you've got to do something. There is something about action that begets more action. If you can't figure out what to do, and you're caught in a confused mental or emotional paralysis, force yourself to *do something*. It really doesn't matter what you do, as long as you start doing. Once you get moving, you'll find it easier to move in positive and thoughtful ways.

I've found that when I'm in the middle of a funk brought on by miserable circumstances or my own failure, I become paralyzed by my own thoughts. One of the most helpful things to do is to do something. Act! Stop thinking and do something! Action begets action. Start moving and you'll quickly feel like moving some more.

And, oh yes, in case you're wondering — in six months I was able to pay off the debt and I began making more money than I had imagined possible. What was an absolutely hopeless and miserable situation changed into one of the most financially rewarding, satisfying experiences of my life.

To implement the ideas in this chapter...

1. Develop a statement of your life's purpose.

2. Look on adversity as a learning opportunity.

3. Develop a system of turning adversity into learning experiences.

Chapter 13
Controlling Yourself —
Part 2: Dealing With Fear
And Adversity

One of the biggest obstacles to the success of any salesperson, yourself included, is fear. Fear reveals itself in a number of ways — any one of which can sap your energy and diminish your success.

First is the fear of rejection, often said to be a salesperson's single biggest obstacle. It's the fear of rejection that keeps you from calling on new accounts or meeting new people within your current accounts. We are all — at some level — afraid that we'll get turned down, and we don't like that feeling.

I recall my first professional sales call. I had to demonstrate a speech therapy machine to a PhD speech pathologist. I had never demonstrated anything to anyone before. I was so scared and nervous that my hands were shaking. On top of everything, my district manager was with me observing! After the call, he asked me if I was aware that I was clenching and unclenching my fist over and over. Evidently, I was so tense that I was not conscious of my actions. That's fear.

Second is the fear of stretching yourself into areas beyond your comfort zone. This fear is probably most common among distributor reps. Most distributor reps have created very comfortable jobs for themselves. You may have also. You have worked hard to create a large group of people who know you, generally like you, and are willing to spend time with you — they are your customers.

Since it's taken you some time to get to this point, you're naturally hesitant to do anything to jeopardize the status quo. That means that it's difficult to push beyond the comfortable discussions you're accustomed to having. You're a little afraid to try some of the techniques I discussed in the section of this book on sales skills.

And this fear keeps you in a rut — stuck in the performance levels you've become used to. Stuck in the behavior patterns that have become comfortable for you.

With most distributor reps, it's not the fear of big things that is the issue, it's the fear of a thousand small things — all related to jeopardizing your fragile hold on your customers and your status quo.

It may be that none of these issues affects you. In that case, great — move on to the next section. But, if you've ever been afraid to try something new in your job, afraid to be held accountable for some level of performance, afraid to stretch outside of your comfort zones, than you need to know how to deal with that fear.

Here's a set of ideas to help you overcome fear and successfully stretch yourself to new levels of productive behavior.

1. Identify the issue. The first step in overcoming fear is to recognize that fear is what you're dealing with. I can remember more than a few miserable hours I weathered sitting at a desk trying to work up the courage to make cold calls. What stopped me was my fear of rejection. And it took several hours of mental games before I realized that fear was the issue. I was afraid.

And, until I realized that fear was the problem, I was powerless to overcome it.

When you find yourself hesitant to do something — particularly if that thing is something new — ask yourself if the real issue isn't that you're afraid.

If you find yourself hesitant to meet new people, present a new product line, or try a new selling tactic, look inward and see where that hesitancy is coming from. If it's fear, acknowledge it, and move forward.

2. Look for deeper causes. Once you've decided that fear is the problem, think about *why* you may be afraid. Have you had a bad experience in the past? Is this a similar experience?

Then, argue with yourself. For example, if you discover you're afraid because of a bad past experience, argue with yourself. Tell yourself that was only one experience, and now you're older and wiser.

This process of arguing with yourself can provide logical support for you to attack your own fear. You can literally talk yourself out of your fear by reasoning with yourself.

Then, you must *act*. The only real antidote for fear is *action*. You must do that thing that you fear. Until you act on your fear you'll continue to harbor it.

3. Remind yourself of past successes. If arguing with yourself doesn't work, remind yourself of a past success you've achieved by doing the thing that you now fear. I finally overcame my fear of cold calling by putting a picture of one of my best customers, a customer I had acquired initially via a cold call, next to the phone. When I felt hesitant to make those cold calls, I'd pull the picture out, and remind myself of my past success in dealing with that fear.

4. Remind yourself of future rewards. What will happen if you're successful at doing this thing you fear? Will you earn more money? Acquire new customers? Provide yourself with a strategic advantage? If so, remind yourself of that thing that you want. You may even put an illustration or picture of it by the phone or in your car where you can be reminded of your goal.

Often, that visual reminder of your future rewards will be enough to stimulate you to action.

5. Remind yourself of past rewards. Have you been successful in the past? Have you enjoyed the rewards of that success? Then remind yourself of some of your past rewards when you find yourself hesitant to do something.

6. ACT! ACT! ACT! Regardless of which of these techniques work for you, the important thing to do is *act.* Sooner or later, you must do something. Until you turn your thoughts into action, you haven't been successful. Ultimately, the only way to overcome fear is to act. All the other things that I've talked about are only means to an end. They are self-management tools you can use to bring yourself to the point where you can act. *Action* is the final victory over fear.

Dealing with Adversity: Learned Optimism

In 1992, Dr. Martin Seligman[1] published a book which may become one of the most significant books of the decade. In it, he describes his lifework. As a research psychologist, Dr.

---

1.   *Seligman, Martin, E.P., Ph.D.* Learned Optimism. *Pocket Books division of Simon & Schuster, Inc. New York, NY 1992.*

Seligman began by studying helplessness in dogs. In an early experiment, he put dogs into a cage from which they could not escape, and subjected them to mild shocks. Later, he put them into a cage from which they could easily escape, and subjected them to the same mild shocks. The dogs would just lay down and give up. Surprisingly, they did not attempt to remove themselves from the irritant. They had learned helplessness and hopelessness.

In subsequent experiments, Dr. Seligman found a similar behavior in human beings. Put into a room and subjected to irritating noises from which they could not escape, they soon learned to give up. When put into a room with a mechanism that would turn off the noise, they still didn't try. They had learned helplessness and hopelessness.

From this beginning, Dr. Seligman continued to formulate a thesis he calls "learned optimism." It says, basically, that human beings learn to have either a pessimistic or an optimistic outlook. Dr. Seligman's book contains a self-assessment to measure the degree of pessimism or optimism of the reader.

Dr. Seligman's thesis derives from the way people explain negative events to themselves. When something negative happens, as it eventually will, the way you explain it to yourself determines your pessimistic/optimistic attitude. There are three components of this "explanatory style."

The first component is the degree to which you believe the event to will be *permanent*. Pessimists believe negative events will be permanent, while optimists believe that they will be temporary.

The second component is *pervasiveness*. Pessimists believe the causes of negative events are universal, affecting everything they do. Optimists believe them to be specific, and limited to the individual circumstances.

The third component is *personal*. Pessimists believe that

negative events are caused by themselves. Optimists believe that the world is at fault.

Here's how this behavioral perspective works in the everyday life of a distributor salesperson.

Let's say you visit one of your large accounts, and your main contact announces that the vice-president for operations has signed a prime vendor agreement with your largest competitor, and that all of your business will be moved to that competitor within the next 30 days. *That's* a negative event.

As you drive away from the account, you think to yourself, "I blew it here. I should have seen it coming. I'm never going to learn this job. I'll blow the next one too. I mismanage them all."

Now, that's a pessimistic explanation of the event. Notice that you have explained it in a way that is personal, "*I* blew it." Your explanation is also permanent, "I'm *never* going to learn to do this job," and pervasive, "I mismanage them *all.*"

Now stop a minute, and analyze how you feel as a result of this explanation. Probably defeated, dejected, depressed, and passive. These are not the kinds of feelings you need to energize you to make your next sales call.

Let's revisit the situation, this time offering optimistic explanations.

The same event occurs — you receive bad news from your best account. As you drive away, you think to yourself, "They really made a bad mistake this time. It's a good thing the contract is only for a year. That gives me time to work to get it back. I'm glad it was only this account and no others."

That's an optimistic explanation because your explanations were not personal, permanent, or pervasive. How do you feel about your future as a result of this explanation? Probably energized and hopeful.

See the difference? The event was the same. The only difference was the way you explained it to yourself. One set of explanations was optimistic, leading to energy and hope, while the other was pessimistic, leading to dejection and passivity.

Dr. Seligman has isolated optimistic behavior as one of the characteristics of successful people. Using various techniques he's developed, he predicted elections by analyzing each candidate's explanatory style. The most optimistic candidates often win elections.

The implications for you are awesome. If you can improve your explanatory style, and make it more optimistic, you'll create more positive energy and hope for yourself, no matter how difficult or negative the circumstances with which you must deal.

Learned optimism can be one of your most powerful self-management techniques.

Here's how to implement it in your life.

1. Analyze your explanatory habits. Wait until you must deal with some negative event or some adversity in your life. Then, stop and observe what you are telling yourself about the event. What do you believe about yourself and the reason why bad things happen? Remember the discussion of "inside-out" from chapter 12? This is where one of those fundamental, "world-view" type beliefs crops up. To what degree are your explanations personal, permanent or pervasive?

2. Note the consequences of your explanatory style. Pessimistic explanations always lead to passivity and dejection. Optimistic explanations always lead to energy and hope. Which is more likely to propel you to future success?

3. If you're pessimistic, you must change the way you think.
Your future success, your ability to achieve all your goals, depends on your ability to rise up and meet adversity with renewed energy and optimism. You can do this by choosing to think differently.

Dr. Seligman makes the following suggestions.

Distract your thoughts. In other words, when you find yourself thinking negative and pessimistic thoughts, tell yourself to "Stop!" You can even say it out loud, or shout it to yourself. Just "STOP" thinking those things. Then, shift your thoughts to something else.

I'd suggest you think about something that brings you pleasure or satisfaction, or something that you're good at.

Dispute your explanations. This is a longer-lasting approach. Argue with yourself. Reason your way out of your negative thoughts. Look at the evidence, or suggest alternatives. Reason from the implications or usefulness of what you're thinking.

Back to our example. On the way out to your car after your miserable call, you're thinking to yourself "I blew it here. I should have seen it coming. I'm never going to learn this job. I'll blow the next one, too. I mismanage them all."

When you catch yourself thinking defeating thoughts, argue with yourself. Think, "Wait a minute, while it's true I may have been able to do something if I had seen this coming, the truth is that the VP would never see me. The other company must have had some special connection. That doesn't mean that this will work anywhere else. It's just this account. There certainly isn't any evidence of this possibility happening anywhere else. And, the truth is that the entire purchasing department is not happy about this course of events. If I stay close to the account, they may find lots of reasons to continue to do business with me."

What you've done is argue with yourself to change your thought processes. As a result of thinking differently, you have more energy, more hope and, therefore, more likelihood of success in the future.

You can change your thoughts. You can choose to think differently. You can choose to believe differently. And that fundamental decision about how you think can, more than any other single decision, affect your future success.

Dr. Seligman has discovered, through his scientific research, a truth that has been known for thousands of years. The Apostle Paul, writing in the book of Romans, counseled new Christians to, "Be transformed by the renewing of your mind." And Solomon said that, "As a man thinks in his heart, so is he."

Your choice of what to think about, and how to think about what happens to you, is one of the most important choices you'll ever make.

To implement the ideas in this chapter...

1. When you recognize that you're afraid,

    • Identify the fear,

    • Look for deeper causes,

    • Remind yourself of past successes,

    • Remind yourself of future rewards,

    • Remind yourself of past rewards,

    • ACT – do the thing you fear.

2. Analyze your *explanatory style.*

3. Note the consequences of your explanatory style on your performance.

4. If you find yourself thinking pessimistically,

    • Distract your thoughts, or

    • Dispute your explanations.

Chapter 14
Working Smart —
Part One: Goal-Setting

I can honestly say that much of my life as a salesperson has been spent in the regular pursuit of the shortcut. That inclination caused me a lot of grief when I was younger and going to school. Taking shortcuts was never the course my teachers recommended. But they were unable to purge that trait out of me, and, as an adult, I continued to search untiringly for the easy way to do everything.

And I discovered that, as a straight-commissioned salesperson, the relentless pursuit of the easiest, best way has paid great dividends. Now, instead of decrying the search for the shortcut as a character flaw, I see it as one of the positive traits of the best salespeople. Only now, I call it something else. Now, I call it *working smart.*

Working smart, defined for distributor salespeople, means thinking about what you do before you do it so you can do the best things in the most effective way. It's the best way to vaccinate yourself from the drudgery of hard work and ineffectiveness.

And, it's a simple process. It's amazing how good you can get — how "smart" you can work — by just spending regular time thinking about what you do.

Let's take this idea of working smart by thinking about what you do before you do it, and apply it to some very specific applications.

Start Smart — Set Goals

One of the most effective strategies to get the most out of yourself is to master the discipline of regularly setting powerful, motivating goals. Goals compel you to work with discipline and concentration rather than going about your job mindlessly and routinely.

This doesn't mean that you can't do your job without goals. You can, and many distributor salespeople do. But the discipline of goal setting forces you to think about what you do. It moves you out of the realm of being reactive — doing what other people want you to do, to being proactive — doing what you want to do.

Once you decide on the most important results you want to achieve, then the only question is, "What is the best way to accomplish that?" The answer to that question leads you to the creation of good strategy. And, once you have created your strategy, you are much more likely to act in a focused, proactive way. You will have thought about the "best things to do in the most effective way." Goal setting is, then, one of the fundamental keys to working smart.

It's much more than just an occasional exercise. Rather, it's a disciplined way of thinking about your job and your life that takes you from being reactive to becoming proactive. Think of it as a mind-set, not a task.

To become effective at it, the goal-setting habit is one which you'll need to build into your life on a regular basis. Every year or so, review and refine your long-term (lifetime) goals and create a set of annual goals. Every few months, review your short-term goals. Regularly create monthly, weekly and daily goals.

Regardless what level you're working on, the process is always the same. Here are the steps you need to master to become an effective goalsetter:

1. Select an area on which to concentrate. This can range from the very deep and foundational, to the very specific and superficial. For example, you may want to focus on something like your spiritual growth. That's a deep and foundational area. Or, you may want to focus on something much more specific, like the state of repair of your home.

2. Select the time period. There are lifetime goals which give purpose and definition to your life. Then, there are long-term goals, which are 8 - 12 years from now. Mid-term goals address the time period from 1 year to 8 years in the future. Short-term goals can be anything from a week to a year.

Let's say that you want to work on annual goals for the financial aspect of your life. You've now identified the area (financial) and the time period (annual). You're now ready for the next step.

3. Brainstorm (Daydream). Next, daydream about what you'd like to achieve with respect to that part of your life. Kick back, relax, and begin to list on a piece of paper all the things you'd like to accomplish in the area that you're working on. Create a list of your dreams. Don't edit or judge what you've written, rather, just make a long list of your dreams.

Nobody else can do this for you because no one really knows your situation and your aspirations better than you do.

Let's say you write these things down:
"Make a lot more money"
"Buy a new car"
"Put aside $2,000 in an IRA"
"Save some money toward's the children's education"
You've created a list of possible annual goals for the financial aspect of your life. Now you're ready for the next step.

4. Prioritize. If you've done a good job daydreaming, you probably have a long list of things you'd like to accomplish. Unfortunately, you can't do everything. You just don't have enough time and energy to do *everything* you'd like to do. So, you must prioritize and select those things that are most important to you.

There's no formula for this, other than to think carefully about each of your daydreams, compare them to your situation, and select those that you feel are the most important to you. Remember to apply a dose of realism to this process. If you want to make $75,000 next year, for example, but you're currently in an $18,000 customer service rep position, that goal may not be very realistic.

Let's say you decide that your two most important goals for the year are "to make a lot more money", and "to save some money for the children's education."

5. Specify. This step requires you to turn your daydreams, which are often pretty vague at this point, into specific, achievable goals.

Let's take the first of the two examples, "to make a lot more money." What's a lot more? After some reflection, you think along these lines: "I made $50,000 last year. If I can increase the business in my territory by 35 percent, I'll make $75,000. While that may seem like a lot, the economy has turned around and it is expanding. I have several customers who are going to invest in major new equipment, and several of my good customers are growing and expanding. If I work hard and smart, I may be able to do it."

Your earlier, vague goal of "making a lot more money," has now been turned into something very specific — "making $75,000 in the new calendar year."

This is a key step in the process because the specific detail of the goal is part of what gives it power. If your goals are vague and abstract, they have less power to shape and direct your behavior.

You should now have a piece of paper with your specific, prioritized goals written on it. When you've reached that point, you're ready for the final step.

6. Refine. Because of the power of a goal to direct your behavior, it's very important that you write your goals exactly as you want them to be. A great deal of your time and effort will be directed toward achieving that goal over the next year. So, it behooves you to make sure the goal is right.

Once you have created written, specific goals, take a moment to apply some criteria to them. See if they measure up to the following questions. If so, good. If not, rewrite them to meet the criteria.

a. Are they specific? Does each goal specify, in detail, exactly what you want to accomplish? Can you make it more specific than it already is?

b. Are they realistic? Deciding to be elected president of the United States may be a worthwhile goal, but it may not be realistic for you. This is where your daydreams meet reality. Your goals should be a stretch and require you to work hard to accomplish them, but they shouldn't be so optimistic that you have no realistic chance of achieving them.

c. Are they measurable? Can somebody else tell if you have achieved your goal? Have you stated it in measurable terms? Back to the example. "To make a lot more money" may be realistic, but it's not measurable. What's "a lot more?" By turning that phrase into a measurable unit, "$75,000," you have made your goal measurable.

d. Do they have a specific time frame? Every goal should have a deadline for completion. That helps put power into it. A goal with no deadline has little motivational power. For each goal, specify the date by which the goal will be attained.

In the example, the goal "To make $75,000 in the next calendar year," has a specific time frame. All the money has to be made by December 31st of that year.

This "refining" step is the last step of the goal-setting process. By the time you have finished it, you will have a written set of goals that express your view of your ideal accomplishments in a powerful, motivational way.

The Power and Purpose Of Goal Setting

Goal setting is the beginning point in taking control of your job (and, in the same way, in taking control of your life). It is possible to go about your job in a purely reactive way. You can visit all your customers on a route-type basis, taking care of their problems and responding to their issues. Your day is determined, not so much by what you want to accomplish, but rather by the problems and demands of your customers.

This reactive, service-oriented mind-set is more common among distributor salespeople than any other kind.

You can do this for years, staying very busy and convincing yourself that you're the critical link in the whole chain. And there's a lot to be said for it.

It is satisfying to take care of a customer's problems. And, certainly, a large part of your job is to respond to your customer's concerns. After all, isn't that a major part of good service?

The problem occurs when you let that mind-set, that mode of working, become your primary mode of operation. When you do that, you've given control of your job and your time over to everyone else.

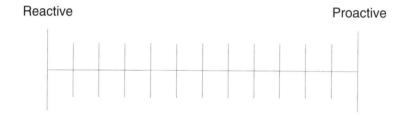

Reactive   Proactive

Illustration #14

Look at Illustration # 14. It depicts a spectrum which describes the styles of doing your job.

At the far left end of the spectrum is the purely reactive style. The person who is purely reactive starts the day with no plan other than to see that day's customers. He has no sales goals — seeking only to respond to what his customers ask for. He mindlessly goes through his days, weeks, months, and years responding only to other people's requests.

On the other end of the spectrum is the purely proactive salesperson. He doesn't bother to check on backorders for his customers because that's outside of his plan. He never takes a phone call because he doesn't want to give up control of his time. Instead, he returns only the important calls on his own schedule. He is the epitome of the proactive style.

Where would you place yourself on the spectrum?

Most distributor salespeople fall to the left of center. And, while being 100 percent proactive may not be the best approach, the more you move from left of center to right of center, the better off you'll be.

Working smart means working your agenda — focusing and directing your behavior in the most effective ways. If you're going to be productive in the Information Age, you must work in the most productive ways. And that means deciding, beforehand, the best things to do. The process of deciding the best things to do is the goal-setting process.

If you look at the spectrum, it's obvious that the fundamental difference between the salespeople on the left and those on the right is the presence of goals. You can't be proactive and work your agenda unless you have an agenda. And that agenda begins with a powerful set of goals.

The first step, then, in moving from reactive to proactive, is creating a set of goals.

Applying the Goal-Setting Process to Improve Sales Results

It's easy to see that you can apply the goal-setting process in an unlimited number of ways. You can apply it to specific, day-to-day activities, like creating goals for every one of your accounts, for example. What do you want to accomplish this year, or this month, in each account? When you answer this question, you've set a goal.

On the other hand, you can apply the goal-setting process to more general, long-range issues, like your long-term financial, social, or spiritual progress.

In any case, it's the first step in gaining control of your time and becoming proactive. The only question is where to begin.

Think back to the onion analogy from Chapter 12. Illustration # 13 illustrates the application levels for goalsetting. You can create goals for yourself at each level of the onion. On the most superficial level are goals having to do with your sales calls and your accounts. Goals at this level are necessary for you to take control of your sales time and become a proactive salesperson.

At the next level are goals for acquiring skills and sales techniques.

The next level consists of goals having to do with your attitudes and personal growth.

Finally, at the deepest level are goals having to do with your purpose in life and your reason for living.

Here's a list, starting from the surface and working downward, of the areas that I believe are worthy of your goal-setting efforts.

- Goals for every sales call

- Goals for every "A" account

- Annual sales, gross profit, and market share goals

- Goals for your sales skills

- Personal learning goals

- Long-term goals for your career, finances, family social, spiritual and physical progress

- An ultimate, "purpose in life" goal

Where you start doesn't make much difference. I've found that you can begin at any level, and move upward or downward as you feel inclined. Sooner or later, however, you should address all the levels.

Review your long-term and annual goals once a year. I believe that you ought to take a day or so every year devoted to nothing but this process. Then, review your "A" account and short-term goals monthly, and write new ones for the coming months. Review your weekly and daily goals each week and each day, and create goals for your sales calls every day.

This goal-setting discipline will put you on the track to focused, directed behavior. And that is the hallmark of the salesperson who is working smart.

Creating Effective Strategy

Goals are a necessary starting point. But they are only a starting point. A goal without a strategy for accomplishing it is practically worthless. Remember, the purpose of creating a goal is to begin the process that culminates in doing the best things in the most effective ways. That's working smart. The first step in the creation of a plan is the development of a goal. The next step is the creation of a strategy to accomplish that goal.

Strategy is another name for a set of actions, or, a plan. When you engage in the process of thinking about what you do before you do it, you inevitably create a plan that encompasses your best thinking about the most effective things to do.

As with goalsetting, there is a process for thinking about strategy that, if followed correctly, will always bring you to the most effective plan you're capable of developing. Once you learn the process, you can apply it to all of your goals — from your lifetime "purpose in life" goal to the next sales call you must make.

The Strategy-Developing Process

The strategy-developing process is a matter of asking a set of six questions of yourself, asking them in the right sequence, and then answering them in writing. The resulting written answers become your plan.

1. Assess the situation. Ask, "What's the situation?"

This step requires you to describe, as accurately as possible, the current situation as it relates to the area that you're thinking about.

Let's consider the example from earlier in the chapter. You've decided to create a strategy to accomplish a goal in regards to your financial situation. So, you describe the salient aspects of your current financial situation like this:

Current income = $47,000
Taxes = $9,000
Savings account = $1,100
Credit card and other short term debt = $5,000
Monthly budget = $3,000

2. Plug in the goal. Ask, "What's the objective?"

Here's where you write in your goal. In this case, write down "To make $75,000 in the next calendar year."

3. Identify the obstacles. Ask, "What will hinder me from achieving the goal?

It's an incredibly powerful process to think in terms of obstacles. The process of identifying and preparing for obstacles will give you incredible confidence and positive power to overcome them.

In the example, let's say that you have identified these obstacles:

- Only three of your current accounts are growing

- Two new competitors are active in your territory

- There are a lot of changes going on in your market

4. Create an overall plan. Ask, "How am I going to accomplish that?"

This is the guts of the process as you consider the best way to reach your goal, taking into consideration the current state of affairs and the obstacles you must face. In our example, let's say you write the following plan.

a. Focus my time on high-potential accounts.

b. Expand my business in "A" accounts by 50 percent.

c. Try to get more manufacturer's reps working with me.

d. Work smarter by spending more time planning and preparing.

e. Open three major new accounts.

5. Identify the materials and tools you'll need. Ask, "What will I need?"

In this step, identify all the tools you'll need. In our example, for instance, you might say:

a. Some forms to help identify the highest potential accounts.

b. A list of high-potential prospects.

c. All the usual sales aids.

d. A list of the names and phone numbers of all the manufacturer's reps in my territory.

6. Create a detailed action plan. Ask "Specifically, what steps should I take?"

This requires you to think very specifically, and to create a "to do" list that precisely identifies each of the steps you'll need to follow, to put them in sequence, and to assign a deadline completion date to each.

In our example, we've arrived at a skeleton plan. Although the final plan would be more detailed than this, the example below is designed to simply illustrate the process:

a. Identify my highest potential "A" accounts. Jan 15.

b. Acquire a list of manufacturer's reps. Jan 31.

c. Create specific account strategies for each "A" account. Jan 31.

When you've finished this simple six-step planning process, you will have created the best plan you're capable of developing. You now have in place a specific strategy for accomplishing your goal, along with a checklist of tasks and dates to measure your progress by.

Applying the Strategy-Developing Process to "A" Accounts.

You can, and should, apply the six-step strategy development process to every one of your "A" accounts at least once every six months. In so doing, you will create a plan for the most effective things you can do. That's smart.

Here's an illustration of how to apply the smart planning process to create a strategy for an "A" account.

1. What's the situation? This question requires you to outline the big picture of the account. What's happening within the organization? What role does your company play? What is this customer trying to do? What changes have occurred recently? What competitors are active with this account?

2. What's your objective? I know you want to sell stuff. But that's too general. In the next six months, what specifically would you like to accomplish with this account? Is it to meet two or three of the key decision makers? To successfully introduce a new line? To increase your commodity business by 10 percent? To increase your gross margins by a point or two? Got the idea? Be specific.

3. What are the obstacles? Specifically, what's stopping you? Is it a well-entrenched competitor? If so, who is it? And to what degree does he have the business? Or is it a less than favorable purchasing agent or department head? Or maybe a philosophy that exists in the organization? The more detailed and specific you can be with your obstacle analysis, the easier it is to create an effective strategy.

4. How are you going to do that? This question requires you to outline your basic strategy. Are you going to low-bid the next project? Are you going to take the purchasing agent out to a ball game? What is your basic strategy for achieving your goal?

5. What specific steps do you need to take to accomplish that? If you're going to meet the corporate executives, you may want to:

- Get their names from the receptionist.

- Ask Bill, your contact, to call them and set up an appointment.

- Fax a short introductory note to them, then follow up with a phone call asking for an appointment.

- When you get the appointment, collect some information to use to present the "systems" proposal.

- Bring Jack, the sales manager, on the second appointment.

Notice that this is a specific list of exactly what you need to do in order to accomplish the objective you described.

6. What do I need? This question asks what materials, literature, help and support you need. Do you need a letter, a copy of an article, some samples, the assistance of a manufacturers rep, the boss's help, etc.? What are the things you're going to need to use to help you accomplish your action plan?

Discipline yourself to ask — and answer — these questions, in this order, for each of your "A" accounts. You'll take a giant step forward in working smart.

To implement the ideas
in this chapter...

1. Set goals for every areas of your life, but especially for your sales performance by using the goal-setting process:

   - Select an area to work on

   - Select the time period

   - Brainstorm

   - Prioritize them

   - Specify them

   - Refine them

2. Focus on these areas of your sales performance for setting goals:

   - Sales calls

   - Sales in "A" accounts

   - Annual sales, gross profit, and market share

   - Learning goals

3. Following the six-step process for creating strategy to reach your goals.

- Assess the situation
- Identify a goal
- Identify the obstacles
- Create the basic plan
- Identify the materials needed.
- Create a detailed action plan

4. Create strategic plans for each of your "A" accounts.

Chapter 15
Working Smart —
Part Two:
Time Management

Making good use of time is one of your "smartest" disciplines. But it's also one of the toughest.

Good time management is more of a struggle for distributor salespeople than for any other type of salesperson. You have more temptations than salespeople in other selling situations. First, there is the temptation to go about your business like a route, mindlessly calling on the same people at the same time every day. Routine calls for no specific purpose are a major time waster.

And then there is the temptation to be so involved in customer service that you have little time left for selling anything. You want to address your customer's backorders and problems, and you legitimately need to intervene at times on their behalf. But, too much of that can be a major timewaster.

Add to that all the paperwork that's required, pile on top of that the countless numbers of manufacturer's reps who want to talk to you, and top it off with the temptation to study new products and new deals all day long, and you have a glimpse of the kind of timewasters that are unique to your job.

All this means that, if you're going to succeed in the Information Age economy, you must be more disciplined and smarter about using your time effectively then ever before.

Time management, for a distributor salesperson, is a daily battle. You will never win the war. It's not like some big deal where, once's it's done, you can look back and see a definite end to it. With time management, you rarely enjoy any kind of major feeling of accomplishment. Time management is not like that. There is no great victory.

Instead, there is a daily struggle. Some days you win more battles than others, but every day you're in the contest.

On one hand, you have all the forces that strive to suck away your energy and time. If you're not careful, you can spend most days being totally reactive. And, while there is some satisfaction in being incredibly busy taking care of other people's problems and concerns, in the end you have only worked everyone else's agenda while abandoning your own.

If you're going to be a successful distributor salesperson, you need to work your own agenda. You need to take proactive control of your day and do the things that you know will be the best things to do. And that requires that every day you fight the battle for control of your time.

Nine Powerful Positive Strategies to Control Your Time

1. Plan precisely for the use of your sales time. "Sales time" refers to the time when you're face-to- face with your customer. It's the fundamental reason for your job. Think about it. There is someone in your company who can do everything else that you do. But, the one thing you do that no one else does is meet with your customer face-to-face. It's the defining moment of your job. It's the part of your job through which you bring value to your company.

Unfortunately, it's very easy to go through the motions of each sales call without taking the time to plan. Most salespeople have only vague sales call plans, if any. From my own personal experience, as well as my experience with the literally thousands of salespeople I've trained, I've come to the conclusion that it only takes three minutes to plan a sales call. So, a daily investment of about 15-20 minutes will provide you with almost all the planning time you will need to thoroughly plan for every sales call.

The results of sales calls that begin with a plan will be far greater than for those that have no plan. Without a plan, it's just too easy to get sidetracked and reactive. When you're finished with the day, you feel exhausted from all the problems you solved and the tasks you completed, but you haven't caused the things to happen that you wanted. So, you've spent your day busy, but ineffective. That's a luxury you can no longer afford.

Planning for the most effective use of your sales time will both increase the quantity, as well as improve the quality, of face-to-face interaction with your customers.

You can apply an abbreviated version of the planning process from Chapter 14 to the discipline of creating powerful sales call plans. Here's how to do it.

- **Start with your objective.** Write down at least one specific objective you want to accomplish today. You'll find it especially helpful to phrase the objective in terms of an agreement you want to reach with your prospect or customer. For example, if you want to present a new product line, your objective might read, "To agree to a trial evaluation of X product line."

Use the words, "to agree to..." as you write your objective. This will focus you on the end result of the sales call by clearly defining it beforehand.

- **Capsulize the one or two major obstacles in one or two words each.** Maybe your customer is often busy and doesn't give you his full attention. Your biggest obstacle might be "distractions." Or, maybe the competition has a long-standing solid relationship in the account. The obstacle might be "competitor's relationship."

  You really don't have to spend a lot of time on this. But, again, the discipline of thinking about and then writing down the obstacles forces you to think strategically about the sales call.

- **How are you going to accomplish it?** Five to ten words outlining your plan in bulleted fashion will do the trick.

- **What do you need?** List the sales aids, samples, literature, documents, etc. that you need to assist you on the sales call.

This process should take you no more than three minutes. Once again, by taking the time to plan first, you will identify the most effective things you want to happen, you will prevent yourself from sliding into a reactive mode, and you will dramatically improve the results of your efforts. Planning for your sales calls is one of the smartest moves you can make.

2. Plan to make good use of uncontrollable downtime. You know what uncontrollable downtime is. It's those times that occur without notice, where your day was turned upside down through no fault of your own.

It's that moment when you've driven an hour to keep an appointment with someone you've been wanting to see, and he called in sick and nobody told you. All at once you're confronted with "uncontrollable downtime." The first temptation is to waste that time.

I learned about uncontrollable downtime the hard way. When I was selling surgical staplers, I often scrubbed with the surgeon who was learning to use the instruments. That's right. I was one of those people in caps, gloves and mask, standing over the patient, across from the surgeon, in the operating room. When they were just learning to use the instruments, surgeons liked to have us there in case they had any problems with the staplers. Most of the surgical procedures in which the staplers were used were major bowel and gastric surgery, and those cases were usually scheduled first thing in the morning, generally at 7:00 A.M.

I was working with a surgeon at a hospital about an hour's drive from my house. Since the case started at 7:00 A.M, I needed to get to the hospital at about 6:30 A.M. so that I could review the procedures and the instruments with the surgeon before scrubbing. That meant I had leave my house around 5:15 A.M. But, since I always made it a practice to bring a box of donuts for the operating room nurses, I needed to leave at 4:45 A.M. to allow time to get to the donut shop. That meant getting up at 4:00 AM.

One of the common practices in a major surgery is to postpone a case if the patient has a fever. The surgical team never wants to add any stress to the patient if the patient has some kind of infection.

You guessed it. Three days in row, as I stumbled into the OR suite at 6:30 A.M., having already been up for three hours, the OR Supervisor glanced at the surgical schedule, looked up at me, and said, "Oh, didn't anyone call you? The case has been postponed!"

On the third day, I decided the uncontrollable downtime

was going to be an occupational hazard of my job and that, instead of becoming upset about it, I should take it in stride by being prepared for it.

Since then, I have always carried some work to do with me wherever I have gone. That way, I'm not frustrated by uncontrollable downtime.

You need to do the same. In your briefcase, always have some literature about that new product to study, or that quote you need to price, or that paperwork to be completed. By being prepared, you're always ready to make good use of uncontrollable downtime.

3. Prioritize your activities every day. In a world that constantly bombards you with things to do, it's incredibly easy and extremely tempting to have your day shaped by the hundreds of demands and requests of everybody else.

I call this the "popcorn" approach to your workday. Imagine a popcorn popper, the old kind with a hot plate on the bottom and a glass canister above it. Visualize the popcorn kernels lying in the bottom of the hot plate, vibrating in the sizzling oil. When it gets hot enough, one of the kernels explodes and careens off the side of the canister and drops back into the oil. A few seconds later another explodes and bounces off a different portion of the canister. And then another shoots off in a third direction, another in yet another direction and again and again. All that energy is dissipated as it shoots off in a countless number of directions.

That's an apt illustration of how some distributor salespeople run their day. Totally reactive to countless interruptions — their energy exploding in a thousand different directions.

The only real way to take control of all these temptations and interruptions is to create a priority list every day, and then stick to that list. That way you have a clear choice between working your agenda or working everyone else's.

If you have no priority list, then the choice is easy — it's always everyone else's agenda that takes precedence.

At the end of each day, before you go home and join your family, take about ten minutes and create a list of everything you want to do tomorrow. Then, go back and prioritize the items in order of importance. Which of all these items is the one which is likely to bring you the greatest result? After that, which is next? Number them in order of importance.

Then, tomorrow, when someone at the office wants you do something, realize that you have a choice. You can do what they want you to do, and that often means not doing what you want to do — or you can work your agenda. Success belongs to the proactive salesperson, not the reactive one.

4. Constantly evaluate the effectiveness of what you're doing. As a straight-commission salesperson, I created a couple of habits that have served me well over the years. One was the habit of asking myself, several times during the course of the day, this question: "Am I doing, right now, that thing that is the most effective thing for me to do?"

I can't tell you how many hundreds or thousands of times my answer was "No." And, every time I answered myself in the negative, I then had to change what I was doing and do that thing which was the most effective. That habit has not only served me well as a straight- commission salesperson, but I find it to be one of my best time management tools as president of my own training and consulting business.

My second habit was to *always do that which is hottest first.* In other words, if I had two or more things to do, I'd always do that thing that was "hottest" first. What's hottest? That's the second part of this habit. Hottest is *closest to the money.*

For example, if I had a choice between seeing one customer

and closing the order, and seeing another to do a product demonstration, I'd close the order. That's closer to the money.

These two habits of daily time management can be powerful weapons you can use in your daily battle.

5. Cluster similar activities. If you have ten phone calls to make, don't make two now, three later, and five this afternoon. Instead, make them all at one time. That way, the amount of time you spend transitioning to the next task will be significantly reduced.

6. Create systems to handle routine tasks. We all have routine things that we must do over and over again. Fill out expense reports, create sales reports, complete other paperwork, file invoices, review back orders, etc.

You'll find that routine tasks can be handled very effectively if you create a system to handle them, and then always handle it in the same way. You only have to think about the best way to do some of these routine tasks once.

For example, if you have to fill out a weekly expense report, always put your receipts in the same portion of your briefcase. Always fill out your form at the same time of the week, in the same place. Again, the duplication of routine efforts make them mindless things. And some things are best done mindlessly.

7. Work effectively with manufacturers' reps. I know what you're thinking. Work with those two-faced, double-dealing, incompetent scum-bags? Yes. Over the years, this was one of the most successful things I did. I learned that, when a manufacturer's rep was active in my territory, if I worked it right, it was like two of me. In other words, every sales call he or she made was like me making one. So, I could double my effectiveness.

Here's what I did.

Every time a new rep came into the territory, I arranged to do a couple of things. First, I tried to find some opportunity for the person. I gave first by creating an opportunity for him.

Then I invited the rep to lunch. I gave him the opportunity I developed, and I got to know him.

Next, I developed a personal profile for that person, and called him several times to pass on opportunities. I let him know that I expected him to reciprocate. Within a few months, the new rep was happy to work in my territory, pretty much as I wanted him to, and refer all the business to me instead of my competitors.

And, every time one of those reps made a call in my territory, it was like duplicating me. Instead of four or five calls a day, I was able to double, triple and quadruple my sales calls by counting every call made by a manufacturer's rep as one of my calls. It's one of the smartest things I did, and one of the primary reasons I was able to build a territory that was five times the size of the average territory.

8. Have two products or lines to present at all times. When I began as a distributor rep, my manager told me that many reps spent all their time reacting to customer's problems and situations. He suggested that I make it a point to always have a product or product line to show on every call I made. Since I thought he knew more about sales than I did, I followed his advice.

But after I began to think about it, I reasoned that as long as I was in front of a customer I should take advantage of that time to sell more product. So, I brought two products and product lines with me, thereby doubling my effectiveness.

I made twice as good a use of my sales time by presenting

twice as many proposals to my customers. I'm convinced that the larger quantity of sales presentations I was able to generate in my territory as a result of these two strategies was a major reason for the success I had.

9. Use an appropriate strategy for the size and potential of the account. Some accounts need more attention than others. It doesn't take a rocket scientist to figure that out. But developing that concept into a workable daily routine is something else.

It means that some accounts should get a visit from you every six months and a phone call once a month. Others get two visits a week.

Don't be afraid to use a phone or fax to keep in contact with your low volume accounts. Invest your time in appropriate methods for the potential of each account you have. Do not treat everyone the same.

Three Negative Rules — Don't Do's.

1. Don't go into the office! It's my number one negative rule. It's based on Kahle's law of office time. Kahle's law is an inviolate observation about nature, that you can count on to the same extent that you count on the sun coming up every day. Kahle's law of office time says this. "If you plan on working in the office for 30 minutes, it will always take you two hours."

There is just something about going into the office that is inherently a time waster. People want to talk to you, you receive phone calls, there's mail to read, coffee to drink, and customer service people to chat with. Add that all up, and it's guaranteed to waste your time.

I once had one of my clients call me and ask about designs for a new office building he was erecting for his business. "What arrangements should I make for the salespeople?" he asked. "Should I build them each their own offices, or should I invest in those modular office systems so that each can have his own workspace?"

I replied, "You should have one phone in a very crowded place. Make it as difficult for them to work in the office as possible. That way they won't come there!"

That's how strongly I believe in this law. Whatever you do, stay out of the office!

But, if you must go in the office, and I recognize that sometimes you must, then go in the last thing in the day, not the first thing in the morning. If you go in at 4:30 in the afternoon with a half hour's worth of work to do, you're much more likely to get it done in 30 minutes than if you attempt the same thing at 8:00 in the morning.

2. Be conscious of time wasters, and work to eliminate them. "Time wasters" are unconscious, time wasting habits you have created over the years. You've become so accustomed to them, that you're probably not even aware of them. So the first step is to become conscious of them.

For years I had an unconscious time waster. Every time I experienced a bad call — something that didn't go the way I wanted it to, I had to find a coffee shop and buy myself a cup of coffee so that I could feel sorry for myself for 15 - 20 minutes. After that short pity party, I was ready to go back at it.

Then, one day, I realized what I was doing. Wasting all that time in a habit that didn't do me any good. I realized that self pity was a luxury I couldn't afford. So I worked to eliminate that habit of drinking coffee and feeling sorry for myself.

I suspect that you may have created some unconscious habits that fall into the category of time wasters. Here's a list I've gathered from my seminars as I've asked the participants to list some of their more cherished habitual time wasters. See if any of these sound familiar:

- Taking smoke breaks.
- Making personal calls.
- Running personal errands on business time.
- Not making appointments — just showing up unexpectedly.
- Small talk with people in the office.
- Not planning your day.
- Reading the morning paper.
- Taking long lunches.
- Eating lunch by yourself instead of with a customer.
- Taking long coffee breaks.
- Being unorganized.
- Trying to do everything yourself instead of relying on your support people.
- Not trusting the system, double-checking everything.
- Not making use of manufacturer's reps.
- Hand delivering paperwork to the office instead of mailing it in.

Got the idea? You may have a special little time waster that you've treasured for years. If you're going to be effective in our time-compressed age, now is the time to work to eliminate it.

3. Don't get caught up in immediate reaction. Immediate reaction occurs when you have your day, or a portion of a day planned, and then you receive a phone call or fax from one of your customers with a problem for you to solve. The natural tendency is to drop everything and work on the problem. After all, isn't that good customer service?

But, when you do that, you become reactive, and lose control of your day. So, isn't there some way to provide service but stay in control?

The problem is the assumption that just because someone calls, their problem is urgent and needs immediate attention. So, you immediately react. But that isn't necessarily true. Often, the situation isn't really urgent, and you can address it later.

All you need to do is ask this simple question of your customer. "Can I take care of it...(fill in the most convenient time for you to do so.)" Sometimes, your customer will say, "Sure, that's OK." On those occasions, you will have gained control of your day back again, and you can proceed with your plan.

Granted, sometimes it is an urgent issue. And on those occasions, you do need to take care of it as soon as you can. But, if you will ask the question, a good portion of the time you'll remain in control.

And, by asking the question, you refuse to get caught up in immediate reaction.

Implement these time management strategies, and you'll make great strides in working smart.

To implement the ideas in this chapter...

Follow these twelve rules for time management:

1. Plan precisely for the use of your sales time.

2. Plan to make good use of uncontrollable downtime.

3. Prioritize your activities every day.

4. Constantly evaluate the effectiveness of what you're doing.

5. Cluster similar activities.

6. Create systems to handle routine tasks.

7. Work effectively with manufacturer's reps.

8. Have two products or lines ready to present at all times.

9. Use an appropriate strategy for the size and potential of the account.

10. Don't go into the office.

11. Be conscious of time-wasters and work to eliminate them.

12. Don't get caught up in immediate reaction.

Chapter Sixteen
Working Smart —
Part Three: Ethics

I can see you frowning right now. "What," you're thinking, "does ethics have to do with working smart?"

That's a good question. I could just as well have put it in the section on relationship building, because maintaining a solid set of ethics is a powerful contributor to positive relationships.

But I prefer to put it in this section because I believe that working under strict ethical guidelines is one of the smartest things you can do. There's a part of working smart that is concerned with making decisions about the best things to do. That's the work you do on goal setting and strategy development. But there's also the portion that's concerned with the best way to *do* those things. Ethics partially addresses this aspect of working smart.

In my first professional sales position, I discovered that honesty and integrity were not just moral imperatives, they were highly-prized qualities that prospects and customers valued. That meant ethics and integrity were also good business.

Everyone would rather work with honest, trustworthy people than with people who are dishonest and untrustworthy. Wouldn't you? If you're going to be someone your customers want to work with, you need to follow a consistent set of ethics. It's smart.

Over the years, I've assembled a specific list of ethical behavior for salespeople that extends beyond the core qualities of integrity. Although there is more to ethical behavior than integrity, integrity is a good place to start. Webster's defines integrity as: "intactness, firmness of character."

It is this *firmness of character* that is the overarching quality that transcends everything you do. It gives shape and substance to the more specific list of ethical commandments that follows. Firmness of character, translated into your sales behavior, means that you do what you say you're going to do, and that you are what you portray yourself to be. In other words, your customers and your colleagues can count on you to act honestly and consistently. They trust you. Trust is an invaluable component of most sales decisions. The salespeople who earn it by being people of character, and people of integrity, have an immeasurable edge over the competition. Working to earn that trust is smart.

Not long ago, I was financing a new marketing project by selling limited partnership investments. I decided to offer these investments to the people who knew me the best, and who were acquainted with my work: my clients. So I organized a number of small investor information meetings with groups of my clients. At one of the meetings, during the informal question and answer session that followed my presentation, one of my clients announced that, regardless of the details of the investment, he knew me to be a man of integrity, and that was good enough for him. Another chimed right in and agreed, saying he had confidence in my integrity also.

I was touched. I told them both that their comment was one of the highest complements they could pay me. Their trust in my integrity sure made doing business together much easier.

Integrity — being a person of solid, reliable character — is the overarching concept for all the specific ethical guidelines that follow.

The Ten Commandments for the Ethical Salesperson

1. Don't intentionally misrepresent anything. Never, never, never lie to a customer. About anything. Period.

2. Fix any important misunderstandings that you can. It's possible that your customer will form incorrect ideas about some of the products you represent or the services that come with them. It's also possible that they will misunderstand things about your competitors, and about the needs and statements of other people who work in their organizations.

It's very tempting, when these misunderstandings work in your favor, to ignore them. However, that's not dealing with integrity. When you become aware of any significant misunderstandings your customer has that impacts the buying decision or the larger relationship, you need to correct them. This doesn't mean that you need to set him straight on his political beliefs or his views on the controversial call in Sunday's football game. But it does mean that, on the important issues that affect the sale, allowing misunderstandings to exist is an act, on your part, of passive dishonesty. Correct them when you can.

3. Work hard for your employer. It's easy for a salesperson to give in to the temptation to cut corners when it comes to working a full day, every day. After all, who really knows if you hit your first call at 9:00 A.M. instead of 8:30 A.M.? And who knows if you take a 30 minute coffee break between calls? And who knows if you make it home by 3:00 P.M. some days, and take a number of afternoons off to visit the golf course or the fishing hole during the summer?

All of these examples are ways of shortchanging your employer that, in all probability, no one will ever know about except you.

And that's my point. *You* will know. A code of ethics is easy to live by when everyone is watching. But it's a real test of character when your ethics are tested in situations where no one else knows, and you know you can get away with it.

You owe your employer consistent, full days of your best efforts. Anything less is unethical.

4. Always be willing to trade a short term loss for the sake of a long-term gain. This may be another definition of integrity — the courage and conviction to walk away from an unethical short-term gain in return for a long-term gain. In other words, always be willing to give up a sale or some immediate advantage if you must stretch the truth or act unethically to get it.

For example, you may have an opportunity to acquire a quick sale because your customer has misunderstood the specifications or features of your product. It's tempting to take the order and not say anything. But that would not be ethical.

The ethical salesperson will correct the customer and lose the immediate gain that the sale would have brought. The payoff, however, is the long-term gain in your reputation for integrity.

A long-term gain achieved ethically is always worth more than *any* short-term advantage.

5. Do what you say you are going to do. This isn't as simple as it sounds. One of the obvious implications of doing what you say you're going to do is that you must not say you are going to do something that you know you can't do. In other words, don't overpromise. That's difficult to do when you're in the middle of a competitive situation over a nice piece of business, and you know the competition is overpromising to get the sale. But, if you're going to be an ethical salesperson, you won't overpromise, because you know you won't be able to do what you say you're going to do.

There's another implication — you must be organized enough to follow through on your promises. The most honest person in the world can be perceived as unreliable if he is not organized enough to follow through on his promises. If you say you're going to call a customer back on Thursday, make sure that you have a tickler file, day-time planner, computer program, or some other system that will remind you to call them back when Thursday comes.

That's being ethical.

6. Give liberally. As a distributor salesperson, you enjoy a challenging job with a lot of freedom and a substantial income level. The world is full of people who would love to have that. You're one of life's more fortunate people.

I think that means that you have a greater than average responsibility to give back to society. Give of your money freely to charitable or religious causes, and give liberally of your time and expertise to the organizations that you can help. Your expertise, your time, your people skills, your organizational skills, and your confidence and ability to get things done — all of these are assets you can bring to the Boy Scouts, your church, the PTA, and a thousand other organizations that can use your abilities.

Since you are more blessed with talent, time, and money than most of the population, you have a greater responsibility to use it for purposes other than just your own edification. Give liberally.

7. Recognize those who help you. It's easy to get into the mind-set that you alone are responsible for your success. After all, you're out there all alone, fighting the battle every day. Nobody else knows what good work you did in getting that account, or how hard it is some days when nothing goes your way.

In spite of this, you couldn't do your job without the support of a whole group of people back at the office. Your manager gave you an opportunity and nurtured you along. The inside people have cleaned up more than a few of your messes, and they positively impacted many of your customers. The manufacturers you represent have put lots of time and energy into creating the products that ultimately provide your livelihood.

All of these people, and probably dozens of others, have contributed in significant ways to your success. It is just as dishonest to not recognize them as it is to misrepresent a product.

The ethical salesperson recognizes those people who have helped him.

9. Never give up. This may seem odd in a section on ethics, but I believe that giving up is the same thing as going home early or taking extra days off without anybody's approval. Both shortchange yourself as well as your employer.

When you give up on a sale prematurely, or you give up on yourself and give into negative thinking, you're choosing to deprive yourself and your employer of the full benefit of your talent and time. That's unethical.

10. Don't speak badly about anyone. In my first sales position, when I was selling amplification equipment, there were 29 major installations purchased in my territory. I got 28. My stomach still gets a little tight whenever I remember one of my crucial sales calls with the # 29 customer.

During the course of the conversation, she stopped me and said, "You know, I really don't like it that you're so negative about your competitor." I was stunned, embarrassed, and flustered. I turned beet red, and stumbled out an apology. But that was the end of that deal.

All because I had spoken badly about my competitor. That was an intensely painful lesson for me. I resolved never to make that mistake again.

As I matured, I realized that, when you negatively judge anyone, you really say more about yourself than you do about the other person. Speaking badly about a competitor, your boss, your company, or a manufacturer, always makes you look bad. And besides, it's unethical.

To implement the ideas in this chapter...

Commit to acting in a 100 percent ethical manner by adhering to these nine rules:

1. Don't intentionally misrepresent anything.

2. Fix any important misunderstandings.

3. Work hard for your employer.

4. Always be willing to trade a short-term loss for the sake of a long-term gain.

5. Do what you say you're going to do.

6. Give liberally.

7. Recognize those who help you.

8. Never give up.

9. Don't speak badly about anyone.

Chapter Seventeen
Self-Directed Learning –
Part One: The Ultimate
Competitive Edge

There was a time only a few years ago that you could achieve a certain level of mastery of your job and, having achieved that competence, you didn't have to worry about getting any better. Those days are gone — swept out by the broom of rapid change.

Because of the rapidly changing environment of these turbulent times, you need to continually learn and improve yourself, or you'll be left behind. In fact, I believe the ability to learn in a focused, systematic way is the ultimate competency — the foundational skill that, if mastered, will eventually lead you to success.

I call this — the ultimate self-improvement skill for turbulent times and beyond — "self-directed learning."

When you hear the word *learning* you're probably reminded of your days in school, or perhaps seminars and company-sponsored training programs come to mind. While these are all means of facilitating learning, they don't capture the essence of the ultimate self-improvement skill.

Self-directed learning is the ability of individuals to absorb new information about the world, and to change their behavior in positive ways in response.

The key is behavior change. Learning without action is impotent. Knowledge that doesn't result in changed action is of little value. Constantly changing your behavior in positive ways is the only reasonable response to a constantly changing world.

Self-directed learning differs from the traditional approaches to training because it requires you to assume complete responsibility for your own behavior change. The stimulus for the learning must come from within you, and you must develop your own learning program to expose yourself to new information, and to change your behavior appropriately.

Let's look at three fundamental areas of a distributor salesperson's job to see how the need to learn is critical.

Products

The explosion in information has led to change and to technological innovation leaping forward at a dizzying rate. This means that new products are coming into the market — every market — more quickly and more regularly than ever before.

Consider what's happened with the product lines you carry. How many product changes and new products did you see last year? Those rapid changes in products are only going to continue at a more accelerated pace.

You can no longer rely on today's product knowledge for a competitive edge. The product that is today's hot new seller will likely become an obsolete dinosaur within a couple of years.

So, you must acquire the skills of constantly learning about new products and new technologies. There will be a continuous string of new terms to master, new features to understand, and new applications to learn. How long ago was it that none of us knew what a "486" was, or what to do with a "CD?" The new products coming at you in the future will make today seem like the slow old days.

Markets

On the other side of the selling equation, markets — your customers — are changing just as rapidly. On one hand, there is a great deal of change in the names and styles of the players (Wal-Mart instead of thousands of independent businesses), while on the other, every industry is becoming more complex as the trend toward specialization creates a kaleidoscope of market segments in place of the homogeneous markets many of us grew up with.

To stay on top of it, you'll have to continually refine your interactive skills and deal with each customer as a unique individual. That will require you to learn more about your customers and the processes which are most effective with them — a never-ending challenge.

At the same time the world is changing rapidly for you, it is changing just as rapidly for your customers. One day it seems that the lowest price is the only concern, while the next day they talk about long-term "partnering" with trusted suppliers.

You'll have to keep up with market shifts, but also with the dramatic changes within each customer's business. You'll have to learn about your customers and markets more rapidly and more thoroughly than ever before.

Processes

The term *processes* refers to the strategies, systems, procedures and tools you use to do your job. The next few years will see incredible changes for you in your sales processes.

Business as usual will fade away. You'll do far more volume with fewer customers, your job description will change, and the tools you use to accomplish these things will also change.

You'll need to become more of a *marketer*, making the decisions about who to spend your time with that I discussed in the early chapters of this book. You'll have to become more of a *businessperson* — organized, logical and focused — as I described in the first couple of chapters of this book. You'll have to become more of a *consultant* — learning more about your customers, and creating partnerships with them based on creative proposals and integration of your systems with your customers'. And, you'll have to become more *technologically proficient* — entering all of your account information and sales call reports on a laptop computer.

Every direction you look, you're faced with rapid changes. And these changes require you, if you're going to stay competitive, to learn and change at a rate never before required of you.

I firmly believe that the ability to take charge of your own learning, to consistently expose yourself to new information, and then to systematically change your behavior in positive ways based on that new information is the *ultimate* competitive edge for the Information Age.

If you can master self-directed learning, you'll eventually master everything else that you need to be successful.

Prerequisites to Mastering Self-Directed Learning

Proficiency at the ultimate self-improvement skill demands some fundamental attitudes on your part. I like to characterize those attitudes as being a "seeker."

A seeker attitude is composed of several parts. First, you must have an attitude of proactive responsibility for your situation. In other words, you must believe that your actions have consequences and that to change the consequences, you must change your actions.

This sounds so fundamental as to be ludicrous, yet it seems to be a concept that is foreign to much of the world's population, who want to blame their problems on forces outside themselves. As long as you remain someone else's victim, you have no responsibility to change your own behavior.

So, you must accept the responsibility for your *own* behavior and for the consequence of that behavior. As one of my clients said to me, "If you always do what you always did, you'll always get what you always got."

That's common sense. But think about the implications of that statement. If you want different results, you must do something differently in order to get them. The responsibility is yours.

Next, salespeople with a seeker attitude need to be open to new information. One of the sure harbingers of pending failure is the attitude that you know it all. Salespeople who continue to improve themselves understand that they will never have *all* the answers. There is *always* something new to learn. And, like magnets, they're continually searching for new ideas, new perspectives, and new information.

Finally, a seeker has the ability to follow through on his plans. *You* must have the ability to act on decisions you make, and to become a creature whose actions arise out of conscious thought rather than unconscious habit.

From time to time, people ask me about the characteristics of my clients. They're expecting me to answer with the size of various companies, or how many salespeople they have, or the product lines they serve. They're always surprised when I answer that my clients are not defined by size or products.

Rather, they are defined by the personality of the Chief Executive Officer (CEO). All of my clients have CEOs who are open minded, interested in outside perspectives, willing to learn, and committed to the growth of their businesses. The salespeople who attend my seminars can be described with the same terms. They're seekers.

It's interesting that this description only applies to a small percentage of the population. It probably describes you, or you wouldn't be reading this book. Take heart in that. In a rapidly-changing world, the competent, self-directed learners will end up on top. The fact that you're probably one of them means that you're already separating yourself from the mass of distributor salespeople who are more interested in maintaining the status quo.

Richard Gaylord Briley, in his book *Everything I Needed to Know About Success I Learned in the Bible,* talks about the 5 percent principle. You're familiar with the Pareto Principle — the 80/20 rule. Applied to distributor sales, the principle says that 20 percent of your customers provide 80 percent of your business, and that 20 percent of the salespeople capture 80 percent of the business. Briley's 5 percent rule is similar. It holds that 5 percent of the individuals in the world provide success and opportunity for 50 percent of the rest of the population. Applied to distributor sales, the Briley rule would hold that 5 percent of the distributor salespeople in the world contribute 50 percent of the volume.

I believe that these 5 percent are active, self-directed learners who maintain the seeker attitude I've described. And I believe that *you* have the potential to be a 5 percenter for the rest of your life. The starting point is the cultivation of the seeker attitude.

Given this set of attitudes, you can begin to master the procedures and disciplines that will characterize you as a self-directed learner and equip you to be successful in our turbulent times.

Core Strategies for Self-Directed Learning

Given the right attitudes, you'll find the following three strategies to be powerful ways to practice self-directed learning.

1. Inject yourself into learning opportunities. There are two parts to the learning equation. The first is to constantly expose yourself to new information, and the second is to change your behavior in positive ways based on that information.

For example, reading this book is a way to expose yourself to new information. That's the first half of the process. If you now make changes in what you do as a result of it, you've accomplished the second half.

The second part rarely happens unless the first part precedes it. That means that you must regularly expose yourself to new information. To do that, you must inject yourself into learning opportunities. You're thinking, "What's a learning opportunity?" It's any event or situation that causes you to face some new information, or that stimulates you to reformat information you already have.

Here are a number of ways to inject yourself into learning opportunities that will help you continuously improve.

- **Read books, magazines and newsletters.** I'm often asked to recommend a book for a new salesperson to read. I usually respond by suggesting that the inquirer go to the library and check out anything that looks interesting. If your attitude is right, you can learn from anything. So, in one sense, it doesn't make any difference what you expose yourself to, as long as you expose yourself to *something*.

Reading any book is better than reading no book. With the proliferation of business books available these days, you can go to the local bookstore or library every couple of weeks and find new books to read.

Almost any book you can find will give you new ideas. Or, at the least, new ways of reformulating things you already know in more useful and practical ways.

In addition to reading books regularly, subscribe to one or more of the sales magazines or newsletters. They make a point of discussing the latest thoughts and presenting contemporary sales situations. There are a number of good magazines and newsletters available.

- **Make use of cassette tapes on sales techniques.** Audio cassettes have the advantage of allowing you to put drive time to good use. Just pop a tape into the cassette player between calls, and you'll be amazed at how many good ideas you can get.

  Many of my clients have created lending libraries of audio cassettes. The company owns dozens of tape programs, and salespeople check them out one at a time, and return them when they're done. I have created several specific programs for this purpose. The one that has the most specific application for you is *How To Become a Master of Distribution Sales.* You'll find an order form for it in the back of this book. Listening to tapes such as this is a way of continually exposing yourself to a powerful body of new information.

- **Attend seminars and workshops.** Seminars and workshops provide you an opportunity to meet with other salespeople and see things from a different point of view — not to mention the material and ideas you garner from the seminar leader.

In some locations, you may have the opportunity to join a learning group. We organize and facilitate a number of these locally. We bring a dozen or so salespeople or CEOs together for a two-hour meeting where we discuss an aspect of sales in detail. The idea is to learn from one another by engaging in a focused, facilitated discussion group.

Add these techniques and personal self-improvement learning situations to your normal product learning opportunities, and you get an idea of the kind of learning commitment you need to make in order to seriously and continually transform yourself.

• **Reflect on your failures.** You're probably thinking, "Where did that come from?" I have learned that *my* failures, both as a salesperson and in my life in general, have provided me with my most intensive learning experiences. I told you about the one sale I didn't get in my first sales position. That's the one I remember most. In fact, I remember all my failures far more vividly then I do any of my successes.

As I thought about each one of them, I discovered what I had done to produce that failure, and I made specific decisions to change to prevent them from happening again.

Personally, I think that this practice has been one of the key reasons for the success that I have enjoyed as a salesperson. You can do the same thing. You are going to fail from time to time. Everyone does. The most important part of failing is taking the time to reflect on the failure and to learn from it.

Be sensitive to all your failures, large or small, and take the time to reflect on them. You'll find them to be potent learning experiences.

2. Question everything. There are two big obstacles to learning that are especially typical of distributor salespeople. The first is "stuck in a rut" behavior. The second is the tendency to over-rely on assumptions. The cure for both is the same: to question everything.

Stuck in a rut behavior evolves out of an attitude that you already know enough. If you're content and smug about your current situation, you're not going to be open to new information. This satisfaction hinders learning because it hampers the motivation to learn. Without the motivation to expose yourself to new information and seriously consider changing your behavior, the necessary changes won't happen. You're stuck in the status quo — oblivious to the need to move out of it.

One of the best ways to pry yourself out of a rut is to begin to ask yourself questions. Question everything you do. Is this the best way to present this product? Should you be calling on this customer once a week? Are you presenting the right solutions? Do you really know your customers as well as you should? Got the idea? The starting point for getting out of the rut behavior is to prod yourself via pointed questions.

The other major obstacle to learning is the tendency to do your job based on unchallenged assumptions. This occurs when you operate on the basis of an assumption that you've never really thought about. For example, you assume that two or three competitors are quoting the same piece of business you are, so you discount deeply. Or, you assume that your customers always know exactly what they want, so you don't take the time to question them.

Unchallenged assumptions cause errors. Because you work on an assumption instead of taking the time to verify it, you make decisions that are inappropriate.

The solution is the same as getting out of a rut. Question everything. From time to time, stop and ask yourself what assumptions you're working on, and then question those assumptions. You'll often find that your assumptions are in error, and the decisions you made that relied on them were also in error.

3. Master a process to change yourself. Taking in information is only half the equation. The other has to do with changing yourself in positive ways. And that's the subject of the next chapter.

To implement the ideas in this chapter...

1. Focus on developing a *seeker* attitude.

2. Inject yourself into learning opportunities like these:

   • Books, magazines and newsletters

   • Audio cassettes programs

   • Seminars and workshops

   • Learning groups

   • Reflecting on your failures

3. Question everything.

Chapter Eighteen
Self-Directed Learning —
Part Two:
The Menta-Morphosis™
Process

Menta-Morphosis is my trademarked name for a special system of self-improvement. Illustration #15 graphically depicts the process.

It's portrayed as a circle, because it must be used over and over again. It's not a one-time task or activity, but rather a continuous way of life. Some of my clients have nicknamed this concept "Kahle's wheel."

The process consists of a number of steps accomplished one at a time in the sequence that they're represented. If you follow each step precisely, and in the correct progression, you'll always improve your performance — it's guaranteed!

Here's how the system works.

Start by Recognizing
Your Need To Improve

This is your entry point into the system. It's the conscious realization on your part that your results are not as gratifying as you'd like them to be. It's the realization that arises out of an attitude I call healthy

**I Need
To
Improve!**

Menta-Morphosis™
The systematic application of your mind to change yourself.

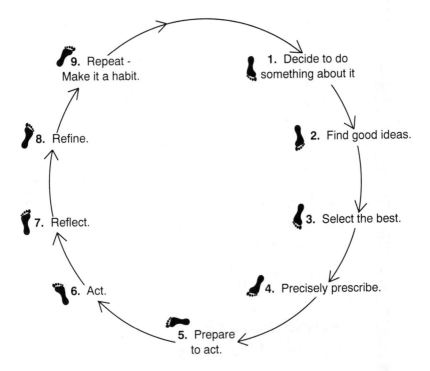

9. Repeat -
Make it a habit.

8. Refine.

7. Reflect.

6. Act.

5. Prepare
to act.

1. Decide to do
something about it

2. Find good ideas.

3. Select the best.

4. Precisely prescribe.

Illustration #15

discontent. Healthy discontent is the beginning of motivation in adults. When you have an attitude of healthy discontent, you either want to eliminate a situation that troubles you, or you want to gain something you don't now have. Without this internal motivation, you won't be sufficiently motivated to stretch yourself out of your comfort zones and develop new habits.

For example, you may be sick of your manager complaining about your lack of new customers. You want to do away with that pain. You're discontent with the ways things are and you want to eliminate that negative nagging pressure.

On the other hand, you may want to add something positive to your life. You'd really like to have a new BMW. Not that your Taurus is a problem. You'd just like to have something that you don't have now. So, your discontent is channeled to a positive thing — gaining something you don't have now.

A little thought at this point will soon make clear the significant role of goal setting in providing motivation to change and improve. When you set a goal, you create healthy discontent. In other words, you create a situation where you want something positive that you don't now have. If you don't set goals, you're reduced to responding to the negative things the world throws at you. You're living someone else's agenda. When *you* set goals, you're living your own agenda.

Regardless of whether it comes from either positive or negative sources, this discontent is the beginning of motivation. Without it, you have no motivation. And motivation is the power that stimulates and energizes the system.

So, the beginning point is your realization that you want to improve to eliminate some pain or realize some gain in your life.

Step One:
Decide to Do Something About It

At this point, you are proceeding on two different levels. One is the general or more cosmic level. You know you need to improve, but you're uncertain in what specific area you should focus. It's OK, at this point, to be vague or general. You'll become more focused later.

On the other hand, you may have a specific need in mind. You know that you want to improve your use of questions, or fine tune your prospecting skills. These are specific areas.

I should point out that, while this system discusses sales improvement and it appears in a sales book, it can be applied to any area of your life. It doesn't matter whether you want to improve your prospecting skills or your parenting skills, your acquisition of new customers or your losing of extra weight — the system can be used for any area of personal improvement.

The first step is to decide to do something about it. I know it sounds very common sense, and it is. But I'm amazed by the number of people who want something better from their lives, but never do anything about it. They see themselves as powerless to change their circumstances or themselves. So, while they continually wish for better circumstances, they don't do anything about it.

My wife and I saw a powerful example of this lack of empowerment a few years ago when we visited Albania, a country that had just emerged from a generation of communist rule. We stayed in the capital city and each morning we would leave with a driver to visit some villages in the country. As we left in the morning we noticed literally thousands of people standing around in the streets and squares — doing nothing. In the evening, when we returned, we saw the same people. Still standing there. Still doing nothing.

In our conversations with them, they were quite resolute in their support of change, and persistent in their hope that their lives would improve. Yet, they didn't see themselves as capable of doing anything about it. They had an image of themselves as powerless to change their circumstances or themselves. It appeared to us that the majority of the nation's populace didn't get to step one.

On a more local level, we all know people who never take action to improve themselves or their situations. My wife is a crisis counselor. She often sees the same people over and over again — people who know what to do to extricate themselves from some situation, or improve their lot. Yet, for one reason or another, they never do. It's the victim mentality. They see themselves as victims — powerless to change their circumstances.

There is probably a little bit of that in all of us. As long as we point the finger at others and blame someone else for our situation, we're powerless to do anything about it. It's not until we see that we have our fate in our hands that we're empowered to do something about it.

If you're going to be successful in changing yourself and improving your situation, you need to make a conscious decision to take your life in your own hands, and do something about it. That's the first step.

Step Two: Find Good Ideas

There are two basic approaches to this, and a virtual limitless number of ways to accomplish it. The two approaches parallel our pain or gain discussion from Step One. You can either identify some problems you want to solve, or you identify some positive behaviors you'd like to acquire.

If you're proceeding on a general level, this is where you begin to focus and sharpen your aim. What problems do you have that you'd like to solve? Make a list.

Then select from that list one or two to start with. Let's say, for example, that your list contains these two sales problems that you want to solve: "Stop wasting time," and "Stop loosing potential new accounts to competitors."

Let's turn these problems into goals or objectives. It's easy. Just rewrite each problem as an objective, beginning with the word "to." So, "stop wasting time" becomes "To stop my wasting time," and " stop loosing potential new accounts to a competitor" becomes "to stop losing potential new accounts to competitors."

Now, let's work with these statements in one more way. Let's turn the negative statement into a positive statement. So, instead of saying I want "To stop wasting time," say, "I want to make better use of my time." And, instead of saying, "I want to stop losing potential new accounts to competitors" say, "I want to gain new accounts."

It's amazing what this little change in language can do for you. Human beings are made in such a way that our minds are much more excited and active about pursuing a potential gain then they are eliminating a problem. Rewriting your statement into a positive objective channels and unleashes your mental powers.

The process of listing problems and then turning them into goals or objectives is one way to program your mind and make it sensitive to new ideas.

But, you can elect to skip this step entirely, and attack the issues on a generic basis. Keep the general need to improve in mind, but don't focus on any specific area.

Regardless of whether you're focused on an objective, or

still generalized, your next step is the same. The next step is to tap into the world of good ideas by intentionally exposing yourself to new information by engaging in a learning opportunity. Imagine a vast cloud that floats just over your head. It's a deep white cloud, sort of luminous, but thick enough that you're unable to see into it. That cloud is the world of good ideas. It's so full of good ideas that you can't see any of them just by looking. You must reach into it with some sort of tool.

You put yourself in contact with the inside of this cloud by intentionally entering into a learning opportunity. That means doing something that will give you good ideas. Recall the discussion of learning opportunities in the last chapter? Go to a seminar, read a book, listen to a cassette tape, watch a video, view a TV program, talk to your boss, or have lunch and conversation with a colleague. The list can go on and on.

You can explore the Internet, reflect on your personal experience, or quite by chance have an experience that makes an impact on you. The important thing is to willfully put yourself into an experience that is going to stimulate your thinking by providing you new information.

Your job now is to refine several good ideas out of that information.

Let's say you go to a seminar. While you're at the seminar, you pick up a dozen good, specific things you can do to change your behavior in positive ways. Or you read a book and, when you're finished, you make a list of all the good ideas you got from it.

The important thing, in both cases, is to make a list of good ideas. Don't worry about editing or judging the relative value of those good ideas yet. Just get them all down on paper. Capture them before you lose them.

At this point, you will have developed a list of good ideas.

You've tapped into the world of good ideas and you have come away with some of it's wealth. It doesn't matter, in one sense, whether you went into the world with a specific objective in mind, or whether you went in with a less clear idea in mind. What does matter is that you end up with a list.

When you've done that, you've completed Step Two.

Step Three:
Select the Best

The easy part is over. If you go no further than this point, and that's what most people do, you've just wasted your time. You're like the person who makes New Year's resolutions but never follows through on them. You're satisfied with good ideas and vague intentions. If you want to get serious, you must progress through the rest of the system.

This step requires you to select some of the good ideas that you wish to implement. I suggest that you look over the list and pick no more than three. Select the ones you believe will have the greatest impact on your performance.

For example, let's say you read a book on sales — this one! As a result, you created a list of good ideas. Your list looks like this:

- Get better organized

- Create account and personal profiles

- Ask better questions.

- Focus on knowing my customers deeper and broader.

- Develop creative proposals.

- Implement "learned optimism."

- Create annual and quarterly personal goals.

- Create monthly strategic plans for my "A" accounts

- Work at continuous improvement.

Now, even I'll admit that this is an ambitious agenda. Realistically, you're not going to be able to implement all of these ideas right away. So, you prioritize by selecting the three good ideas that you think will have the greatest potential effect on your performance.

After some thought, where you soberly consider your own strengths and weaknesses, you select these three:

- Get better organized.

- Ask better questions.

- Create monthly strategic plans for my "A" accounts.

These are the three ideas you're going to focus on. What about the rest? Are they worthless? Not at all — they're just not the highest priority at this moment. Create another file for yourself. Label this one, "Good ideas." Then put your list and all the supporting notes for those ideas into that file. When you've completed "Kahle's wheel," and you have successfully implemented your current high priority list, they'll still be there for you to consider again.

When you've gotten to this point, you've successfully completed Step Three.

Step Four:
Precisely Prescribe

Now, take your three high-potential ideas, and turn them into "precise prescriptions." This is the step that separates the men from the boys, the adults from the children. This is hard work. This step requires you to move from good ideas and vague intentions to specific commitments to change your behavior in precise ways.

Here's what you must do. Translate each of your good ideas into *precise prescriptions* by rewriting them, beginning with the words "I will..."

In the example, let's work on the good idea, " Ask better questions." Rewrite it to read, " I will ask better questions." You'll have to admit that this statement is quite vague. Will you ask better questions all of the time? Of all your customers? Of all your prospects? And, what exactly is a "better question?" Who is going to decide that it's better? The vague intention "I will ask better questions," needs to be made more specific.

As you think about exactly what you mean, and the point in the sales process where questions will render the most positive effect, you decide to rewrite the statement to read, " I will ask better questions to help me understand a customer's Gap before I make a presentation."

That's much better because it's more specific. But you're not home yet. Now, rewrite it again. This time making sure that it meets two criteria:

- It expresses behavior that someone else can witness.

- At the end of the day, you can ask yourself whether or not you did what you said you were going to do, and you can answer that question with a simple "Yes" or "No."

Let's go back to the example.

You have written the statement, "I will ask better questions to help me understand a customer's Gap before I make a presentation." Does that express behavior that someone else can witness? Can a tiny, invisible sales manager who rides around on your shoulder all day witness you do that? Not really, because someone else couldn't judge what "better" means. You need to define exactly what you mean.

So, you rewrite your statement again. This time it reads like this, "I will ask three questions that reveal a customer's Gap before I present any new proposal." That's better. Someone else could determine whether or not you asked three questions. And "reveal a customer's Gap" is more objective than your previous statement. An invisible sales manager riding on your shoulder could witness you do that, and determine whether or not you did what you said you were going to do. So, your statement now meets the first criterion.

Now, consider your goal in light of the second criterion. Is it something that, at the end of the day, you can ask yourself "did I do this," and answer yes or no?

In this case, probably *not,* because you haven't said if you're going to do this with every customer, or with only a few of them. So, you rewrite the statement one more time. This time it comes out like this: "I will ask three questions that reveal a customer's Gap prior to every new proposal I present."

At the end of the day can you say "Yes," I did it, or "No" I didn't? Yes. So, now your statement meets the second criterion.

Congratulations. You've succeeded at the crucial step of translating your good ideas and vague intentions into precise prescriptions for your future behavior. You've completed one of the most difficult tasks in my system. You're now ready for the next step.

Step Five:
Prepare to Act

Prepare to do what you said you are going to do. If you're going to ask at least three good questions, perhaps you should prepare those questions in advance. You may need to collect some literature, purchase some supplies, gather some information from the office, and so on. Before you can act, you need to fully prepare yourself so that you have no obstacles in the way of changing your behavior.

Step Six:
ACT!

This is often the hardest thing to do. Now you must actually stretch yourself and do something that you may never have done before. You'll push yourself outside of your comfort zone to the risky area of behaving in some new way.

This is almost always difficult and laden with fear and anxiety. You'll make the task easier by following the Menta-Morphosis process to this point. Doing so will establish the logical reasons to change and try something new. It will also define your new behavior very precisely and thus make it easier to do. You've stacked the deck on your side to make it easier for you to improve.

You may, however, find it difficult to motivate yourself to do the thing you're committed to doing. If so, you'll find it helpful to reread Chapter 12 and use some of the techniques discussed in it for managing yourself.

The tool illustrated in Illustration # 16 can be a very helpful motivator. Here's how to use the Sales Habit Builder.

Write the current month in the space provided. Then, take each one of your precise prescriptions and reduce each to a single code word. For example, the "asking three questions" prescription could be reduced to the single word "questions." Write each of these words on one of the lines in the right hand column marked "Activity."

Now, at the end of each day, ask yourself this question for each of your prescriptions: "Did I do, today, what I said I was

Sales Habit-Builder

From time to time, you'll discover certain activities that are so helpful to you that you'll want to make them habits. Use this chart to keep track of your progress. List the activity in the column on the left, and then put a check mark in the column for the date on which you engaged in that activity.

Month: _____

Activity	1	2	3	4	5	6	7	8	9	10	11	12	13	14	15	16	17	18	19	20	21	22	23	24	25	26	27	28	29	30	31

Illustration #16

going to do?" If you can honestly answer "Yes," then mark an X in the space for today's date. If the answer is "No," then put a zero in the space.

This little tool will keep your prescriptions firmly planted in your mind, and keep you focused on making the changes you said you were going to make.

When you have acted by doing the things that you said you were going to do, a number of times, then it's time to move on to the next step.

Step Seven:
Reflect

Reflection is simple enough. It merely requires that you think about what happened and that you learn from it. Ask yourself these questions, and then write down the answers.

- Did I do exactly what I said I was going to do?

- If not, why not?

- How did it go? What good things happened as a result? What happened that wasn't so good?

When you have analyzed your new behavior, you have successfully completed Step Seven.

Step Eight: Refine

Now that you've reflected on the experience, you can refine your action. This step is very similar to Step Five, where you wrote precise prescriptions. Only now, you're going to change your prescription based on your experience in the real world. So, rewrite your prescription to reflect your experience and your need to implement this good idea. For example, you may find that asking good questions has had excellent results, but you found it somewhat strained and artificial to ask everyone the same three questions. You decide, therefore, to ask four or five questions, but to create a larger menu of 10 or 12 to choose from.

You rewrite your prescription to read like this: "I will ask at least 4 or 5 good questions that reveal a customer's Gap (selecting them from a prepared menu) prior to every new proposal I present."

Just like the original prescription, judge these statements by the same two criteria we discussed in Step Five. Then you're ready for the final step.

Step Nine:
Make it a Habit

To make this new behavior a habit, you'll need to repeat it at least 20 or so times in a relatively compressed period of time. In other words, don't let those 20 repetitions stretch over the next 24 months. Rather, try to get to them in the next 30 days. That's what your habit builder chart is for. Keep track of your progress every day, until you're doing the new behavior unconsciously. You will go from unconscious incompetence to unconscious competence. In other words, you will create a new, positive habit.

Congratulations, you've significantly improved your performance.

Notice, however, where that brings you in the Menta-Morphosis circle. Back to the starting point! That's right. Now it's time to begin all over again.

That's where your file of good ideas comes into play. If you're regularly injecting yourself into learning opportunities, and regularly collecting good ideas, you'll constantly be working at improving yourself. And that means that your success is just a matter of time.

To implement the ideas in this chapter...

Follow the nine-step process for establishing positive habits.

1. Decide to improve.

2. Find some good ideas.

3. Select the best of them.

4. Write precise prescriptions for yourself.

5. Prepare to act.

6. ACT!

7. Reflect on your experience.

8. Refine your behavior.

9. Repeat the behavior until it's a habit.

Chapter Nineteen
Nine Power Strategies for Distributor Salespeople

If I could step back and look at the key strategies that would summarize the concepts, principles strategies, and tactics I've discussed in this book, my list would look like this.

1. Focus On Results

At first, you may think this to be common sense and self-evident, and to some degree it is. However, many distributor reps are guilty of "going through the motions" selling. In other words, you see Customer A on Tuesday morning because that's your habit. Instead of being driven by the objective you hope to achieve in that meeting — the results — you're driven by habit. You go where it's most comfortable rather than where it's most effective.

You can apply this strategy in almost every aspect of your job. If you focus on results, you rank your prospects and customers in terms of their potential and spend the greatest amount of your time with the highest potential accounts.

Create specific call objectives for every call, and annual objectives for every one of your key accounts — focusing on the results you want to achieve.

View the products and customers you choose to invest your time into in the same light. Which products will bring you the best results? Those are the ones you promote, if you're focusing on results.

Manage your time and territory precisely, asking yourself daily, if not hourly, "What is the best use of my time right now?"

Put all this together and the words "FOCUS ON RESULTS" become an overarching strategy that affects everything you do.

2. Get Important!

Get important to your customers, and get important to the manufacturers whose products you represent.

In this rapidly-changing world, new sources of competition are constantly surfacing. It seems that pressures on price and margin never stop. In this kind of environment, how can you secure a spot for yourself that provides you a good income and some security?

The secret is to *get important.* When you're important to your manufacturers, you're able to provide them the one thing they need from you. Access to your customers. Think about it. They can warehouse and ship and bill their products almost as well as you can. What they can't do as effectively as you is get in front of your customers.

It's always going to cost them more to get to your customers because they have a limited number of products over which to spread their sales cost, while you can spread your costs over a much wider number of products. Thus, you should always be able to access the customer at a lower cost than the manufacturers. And, the smart ones know that. So, your ability to get important to your manufacturers is directly dependent on your ability to provide them access to your key customers.

That means that you're going to have GET IMPORTANT to your customers. You do that by becoming, in your customer's mind, an integral, almost indispensable, part of his business. You can't do that if you restrict your activities to quoting the lowest price and picking up orders. Rather, you must systematically create relationships with the most important people within your key accounts, invest your time in learning about their business and getting to know them better than anyone else, and then providing creative solutions and systems that solve deep and systematic problems. When you do this consistently and effectively, you become, in the eyes of your customer, a valued part of your customer's business. And that makes you important to them.

3. Think A Lot

It's easy to do your job by mindlessly going through the motions. You see the customers with whom you are comfortable, quote the stuff they ask you to, grumble about the paperwork, and complain about price competition.

That's easy. Unfortunately, it's also a prescription for eventual failure. The world is changing too rapidly today to do your job mindlessly. Your customers are changing, products and vendors are changing and adapting, new competitors and technologies are springing up. If you go through your job mindlessly, you'll soon be outdated and ineffectual.

Do just the opposite. Commit yourself to the challenge of continuous improvement. Think about everything you do and examine ways to improve and wring more value out of it.

Challenge and question everything you do. Is this the best way to write up a quote? Should you be visiting this account, or would the other one hold more potential? Should you really be spending your time promoting this product, or is another one important? Should you really be lunching with this customer or should you invest your time in another? Is this the best way to file your old quotes, keep track of customer contacts, and file product literature?

Got the idea? Never rest. Be discontent with every aspect of your job to provide the stimulation to improve it. Think a lot.

4. Master the Art of Asking Questions

There is no one thing you can do that is more powerful than asking a good question. You know that from reading Chapter 10. But, with the risk of being redundant, let me emphasize again that asking questions is the single best thing you can do.

When you ask good questions it does several things:

- It builds relationships by conveying the feeling that you are sincerely interested in the customer.

- It helps you to understand the customer better, and thus equips you to provide effective solutions to his needs and interests.

- It conveys the perception of your competence.

- It uncovers opportunities.

- It clarifies issues.

Once again, asking good questions is the single most effective thing you can do.

5. Sell A Lot!

Wait! This isn't as blatantly obvious as it seems. When I say "sell a lot" I don't mean to create a lot of invoices and get lots of pats on the back by the boss, although that certainly is a good thing to do. I'm talking about something much more specific than that. I'm talking about the quantity and quality of sales presentations you make. Picture a distributor salesperson who goes through the motions — visiting his customers, picking up orders, talking about back orders and problems, and occasionally discussing a piece of literature on some product line. Now, contrast that person with another distributor salesperson who always has one or two products to discuss and present to every account, and who doesn't see anyone without suggesting, demonstrating, or presenting some product, service or program. The difference between the two salespeople is the *quantity of sales presentations.* Which of the two do you think will be more successful?

That's a no-brainer question. Sell a lot means to concentrate on increasing the quantity of your sales presentations. Here's a telling little exercise. Keep track, every day for one week, of the number of times you present a product, program or service to your customers. Just the quantity of sales contacts. It may surprise you. Now, next week, see if you can double that number. That also may surprise you because you'll find how easy it is to increase the quantity of sales contacts with a little planning and preparation.

Do so, and you'll increase your sales effectiveness.

6. Continually Peel the Onion

No, this didn't get mixed up with the cookbook manuscript. Remember the onion analogy that I've used several times throughout the book? It basically says that most salespeople deal with their customers in superficial ways. As long as you're satisfied to maintain a superficial relationship with your customer, you're vulnerable to competitive pressures, and you'll never reach your full potential.

If you want to sell successfully in our turn of the century environment, you need to continually peel back the layers and achieve deeper understanding and relationships with your customers.

That means digging deeper to understand them better, continually working to present deeper programs and services, and using every encounter to uncover deeper layers of truth.

You must use discipline and technique to go deeper with your customers. Deeper knowledge, deeper relationships, and deeper solutions. Your courage in digging deeper and peeling back the layers of the onion will separate you from your competition. But you must be courageous, skillful and dedicated to continually *Peel the Onion*.

7. Become A Chameleon

People like people who are like themselves. People buy from people they like. People buy, therefore, from people like themselves. Therefore, be like them. Treat each of your customers the way he wants to be treated. The Apostle Paul, writing in the Bible, said "I have become all things to all people in the cause of Christ." We're not talking about anything so important as spiritual issues here, but the principle still applies. Every one of your customers is comfortable dealing with people in a certain way — they are more likely to buy from people who they are comfortable with. Study each decision maker, and respond to him or her in the way in which he or she wants to be treated.

Remember the chameleon. It is unique in its ability to change colors to blend into its environment. Learn to do the same things. It's one of the skills of the best salespeople.

8. Work Smart!
Prioritize and Strategize Everything

Spend at least 20 percent of your work week planning and preparing for the other 80 percent. Create powerful lifetime, annual, monthly, weekly, and daily goals. Prioritize your accounts, your time, your prospects, the products you represent, your territory, and so on. Constantly think about the most effective things to do, and concentrate on doing them in the best way. Never rest in your quest for the better way and the more effective thing to do.

9. Dedicate Yourself to
Continuous Improvement

Unfortunately, just a few years ago you could get good at something, and then coast for a while. Not anymore. You're never good enough. As soon as you gain mastery of an aspect of your job, the goal changes, the environment transforms itself, and you must relearn.

I'm convinced that the single most important success skill in the turn of the century environment will be your ability to learn and transform yourself. It's not a one-time task, or something you stop doing in school. Rather, it's a continuous, life-long challenge. You must continually improve, in every area of your job, or be left in the dust of those who do. It is the ultimate competitive strategy, and the one that transcends all the others.

To implement the ideas in this chapter...

Implement the nine summary strategies for distributor salespeople:

1. Focus on results.

2. Get important.

3. Think a lot.

4. Master the art of asking questions.

5. Sell a lot.

6. Continually peel the onion.

7. Become a chameleon.

8. Work smart by prioritizing and strategizing everything.

9. Dedicate yourself to continuous improvement.

Notes:

Notes:

To Order Additional Books...

Order additional copies of *How To Excel at Distributor Sales* for each of the salespeople in your company.

# Copies	Price Ea.	Plus shipping & handling
1 - 10	$34.95	$ 3.50
11 - 30	$31.95	$ 7.00
31 - 60	$29.95	$12.50
61 - +	$26.95	$18.50

Mail To: The DaCo Corporation
PO Box 230017
Grand Rapids, MI 49523
Or, Fax To: (616) 451-9412

- -

Please send me the following copies of *How To Excel at Distributor Sales*

Quantity _____ x Price Each _____ = Total Price _____

Shipping and Handling _____

Add 6% Sales Tax _____
(Michigan Only)

Total _____

☐ Bill my credit card #_____ Ex. date _____

Circle one: Mastercard   Visa   American Express   Discover

☐ I've enclosed a check

Name _____

Signature _____

Ship to: _____

Name

_____
Company

_____
Address

_____
City   State   Zip

_____ _____
Phone   Fax

Other Productivity Tools From Dave Kahle

Audio Tape Programs

How to Become a Master of Distribution Sales $139.50

A concise, easy to follow tape program designed to help you attain the level of sales success you may have thought impossible. The program is packed with seven hours of powerful material, and it comes complete with a comprehensive guide. Ten audio cassettes and a 65 page reference manual.

Leader's Guide $65.00

Organize the audio cassette program into a series of 4, 6, or 10 small group sales training meetings with this how-to-guide.

How to Find, Interview, Select, and Hire a Good Salesperson $97.50

Take the guess work out of your next hiring decision with this comprehensive tape program. This is the most extensive step-by-step guide you'll find. Four audio cassettes and a 70 page reference manual.

How to Use Telemarketing to Add Profits to Your Distribution Business $69.50

A step-by-step, easy to use guide to help you make a decision about the feasibility of using telemarketing, and then create and implement a telemarketing department. Loaded with actual examples from other distributors. Four audio cassettes and a 65 page reference manual.

Sales Force Software

The Ultimate Sales Productivity System.

This sales force software has been designed exclusively for distributors. Automate your sales force, simplify account records and sales call reporting, provide detailed market information, create on-line sales forecasts, reduce paperwork, streamline communications and organize your accounts - all with one powerful productivity tool.

Self Study Manuals by Dave Kahle

Each segment of the "Sales Mastery Series" comes complete as a concentrated course of it's own. Ideal for specific areas of targeted growth.

Handling Objections $ 14.50

Systematically Improving Performance $ 14.50

Time and Territory Management $ 14.50

Send orders to:

The DaCo Corporation
PO Box 230017
Grand Rapids, MI 49523

1-800-331-1287 • Fax: 616-451-9412

E-Mail: Daco19@AOL.com

Dave Kahle is available to:

- Speak at your conference or convention.

- Create customized sales training programs for your outside sales force, inside sales force, or sales managers.

- Provide "How To Excel at Distributor Sales" seminars.

- Consult with you on issues relating to sales productivity.

For more information:

Call: 1.800.331.1287

Write: The DaCo Corporation
PO Box 230017
Grand Rapids, MI 49523

Fax: 616.451.9412

E-Mail: Daco19@AOL.com

About The Author...

Dave Kahle is recognized as the national expert on sales productivity for distributors and dealers.

He has acquired his message through real life experience. As a distributor salesperson, Dave took a new territory to over $5,000,000 in sales in five short years, becoming the number one salesperson in the nation for that company.

As a general manager for a division of a distribution company, Dave directed that company's growth from $10,000 in monthly sales to over $200,000 in just 38 months.

Dave annually presents over 100 seminars and training programs on systematic approaches to sales, marketing and self-directed learning. He routinely publishes on those topics in trade journals and sales and marketing publications.

He holds a B.A. degree from the University of Toledo, and a Master's from Bowling Green State University.

He and his wife live in Grand Rapids, MI, where he is a father, step-father, adoptive father, a foster father, and a grandfather.

Dave is a member of the National Speaker's Association, The Author's Guild, and the Christian Businessmen's Committee.